Movement: Onsta

Movement: Onstage and Off is the complete guide for actors to the most effective techniques for developing a fully expressive body. It is a comprehensive compilation of established fundamentals, a handbook for movement centered personal growth and a guide to helping actors and teachers make informed decisions for advanced study.

This book includes:

- fundamental healing/conditioning processes
- essential techniques required for versatile performance
- specialized skills
- various training approaches and ways to frame the actor's movement training.

Using imitation exercises to sharpen awareness, accessible language and adaptable material for solo and group work, the authors aim to empower you the reader to unleash your extraordinary potential.

Robert Barton is University of Oregon Professor Emeritus of Acting, whose publications include the books: *Acting: Onstage and Off* (Wadsworth Cengage), now in its seventh edition and one of the most widely used acting texts; *Voice: Onstage and Off* (with Rocco Dal Vera; Routledge), now in a revised and expanded third edition; *Acting Reframes: Using NLP to Make Better Decisions in and out of the Theatre* (Routledge); *Theatre in Your Life* (with Annie McGregor; Wadsworth Cengage), now in its third edition, a genuinely multicultural guide to theatre on a global level, featuring African and Asian theatre as well as American ethnic performance; *Life Themes* (Wadsworth Cengage), a companion anthology; and *Style for Actors: A Handbook for Moving Beyond Realism* (Routledge), which guides performers in the acting demands of Greek, Shakespearean, Restoration and Eighteenth Century, and other plays that move outside realism into "stylization," recipient of the Best Book Award from the Association for Theatre in Higher Education. Robert is also the editor and adapter of a new edition of *The Craft of Comedy*, originally written by Athene Seyler and Stephen Haggard.

Barbara Sellers-Young is a global expert on movement for the actor and is Emerita Professor in the Dance Department and former Dean of the College of Fine Arts at York University, Toronto. Prior to York University, she was Chair of the Department of Theatre and Dance at University of California, Davis, where she was also the head of the movement curriculum for the MFA program. Her publications include: *Oxford Handbook of Dance and Ethnicity* (edited with Anthony Shay; Oxford University Press); *Embodied Consciousness: Performance Technologies*, (edited with Jade Rosina McCutcheon; Palgrave Macmillan); *Breathing, Movement, Exploration* (Applause); and *Teaching Personality with Gracefulness: Transmission of Japanese Cultural Values Through Traditional Dance Theatre* (University Press of America). She is a recipient of the Dixie Durr Award for service to dance research from the Congress of Research in Dance and a Distinguished Alumna Award from the School of Music and Dance, University of Oregon.

Movement

Onstage and Off

Robert Barton and Barbara Sellers-Young

Routledge
Taylor & Francis Group
NEW YORK AND LONDON

First published 2017
by Routledge
711 Third Avenue, New York, NY 10017

and by Routledge
2 Park Square, Milton Park, Abingdon, Oxon OX14 4RN

Routledge is an imprint of the Taylor & Francis Group, an informa business

Library of Congress Cataloging in Publication Data
Names: Barton, Robert, 1945– author. | Sellers-Young, Barbara, author.
Title: Movement onstage and off / by Robert Barton and Barbara Sellers
Young.
Description: New York: Routledge, 2017. | Includes bibliographical
references and index.
Identifiers: LCCN 2016024906 | ISBN 9781138907812 (hbk: alk. paper)
| ISBN 9781138907829 (pbk: alk. paper) | ISBN 9781315694887 (ebk)
Subjects: LCSH: Movement (Acting)
Classification: LCC PN2071.M6 B37 2017 | DDC 792.02/8—dc23
LC record available at https//lcc.loc.gov/2016024906

ISBN: 978-1-138-90781-2 (hbk)
ISBN: 978-1-138-90782-9 (pbk)
ISBN: 978-1-315-69488-7 (ebk)

Typeset in Univers
by Keystroke, Neville Lodge, Tettenhall, Wolverhampton

Dedication

To our spouses

Carol Barton

and

Jade Rosina McCutcheon

With love and gratitude for not only putting up with us during the research and writing of this text, but for actively helping us accomplish those tasks.

Contents

Illustrations

Preface

This book will help you move. It joins *Acting: Onstage and Off* and *Voice: Onstage and Off* and takes their perspectives and formats into the area of movement for actors. It does not, however, require reading those books to engage with this one as it also functions independently. The three all aim to address their subjects as both theatre skills and personal ones, aiming to assist you to become a better actor while also learning to act your own life better. *Movement: Onstage and Off* focuses on the workings of the body in and out of the theatre, the crucial component in which your first impression is often your last.

There is more content than can be thoroughly covered in a single class or a few months working independently and this is intentional because *Movement: Onstage and Off* is your lifelong guide to all matters regarding the use of your body in performance contexts as well as social interactions. It will take you far beyond your physical past and present and into your projected future. As various questions or challenges come up during the rest of your training, during your career and during the full arc of your personal life, you will be able to return to this volume for help. Even your search for other texts can start here.

The book is a guide to the most effective techniques for developing a fully expressive body. It can serve you equally if you are a reader alone or as one taking part in class/rehearsal, since it is formatted to be accessible for independent or group work. No readers will feel excluded or unable to participate fully.

The book is not competition for any other text or system, but rather a compilation of established fundamentals, a handbook for movement centered personal growth, and a guide to helping actors and teachers make informed decisions for advanced study. The chapters are largely stand alone and do not require cumulative reading.

The onstage/offstage perspective has continued unique among acting books. Acting teachers are always faced with the question "How can we prepare acting students to enter the profession with the largest unemployment rate in the world without offering them crucial life skills for whatever other jobs they pursue?" These three books answer that question and offer concrete life strategies. *Movement: Onstage and Off* covers the full spectrum of movement for the actor as performer, while also fully examining that of the actor as functional interactive human being.

Movement texts tend to fall into the following categories: general overview approaches to acting, physical theatre methods, **mask, mime and related concepts**, combat approaches with and without weapons, somatic approaches, period style acting texts with significant movement focus, embodied cognition works based on neuroscience, and body language/kinesics guidebooks and intercultural integrations of Asian aesthetic conceptions into actor training. These texts either stay in the realm of theory rather than practice, fail to focus directly on the work of the actor, devote only a portion of the manuscript to the subject area, or are highly specialized rather than comprehensive.

Movement: Onstage and Off differs from others available in the subject area in that:

1. It is **easy to understand**. Our highest priority here is to speak to the reader without intimidation or confusion.
2. It **links theatre and life**, rather than isolating them, so working on oneself as a person can happen while acting and vice versa.
3. It **considers all causes and effects**. It addresses psychological blocks to progress as well as the physiological.
4. It **uses imitation exercises** to sharpen awareness. Believing that imitation is indeed the highest form of flattery, the authors encourage actors to serve as each other's "physical mirrors" to increase the depth, detail and caring involved in movement growth.
5. It presents material that is **highly adaptable**, used alone or as part of a group, with both solo activities and ensemble projects on which class members can collaborate.
6. It **aims to empower**. It takes the position that each of us has extraordinary potential waiting to be unleashed and each teacher has the potential to guide this freeing of range.
7. It **honors all approaches** rather than indoctrinating and imposing bias. It provides a "consumer's guide" to advanced study and the many other books out there, comparing and contrasting, and offering shopping tips.
8. It tries to make an undeniably challenging and potentially intimidating subject enjoyable. While not denying the hard work aspects of movement training, it also **encourages fun**.

The text is of interest to graduate level scholars, to undergraduates, as well as freelance actors and directors employing it as a resource, with equal usefulness to academics and professionals, as well as anyone interested in pursuing the actor's craft.

Working alone: One of the advantages for the solo reader is being able to work entirely at your own pace, repeating any activity until you feel it has been mastered. The "stay open" design of the cover allows reading a passage with one's hands free to execute an activity. Partnering: As anyone who has embarked on an ambitious fitness program can attest, it can be a great bonus to have a work-out "buddy" to keep you motivated and provide feedback.

The arc of the book starts with an acute analysis of the actor's past influences and current condition. It then moves from healing/conditioning processes through various training approaches and essential techniques required for versatile performance, then transitioning to specialized skills (such as those required in various stylized plays) and ending with suggestions for ways to frame the actor's movement training/future maintenance.

Chapter Overview

Chapter 1 Body Ownership

Analyzing individual movement histories and tendencies for deeper self-knowledge

Chapter 1 affirms that actors already know quite a bit about their bodies and helps organize that knowledge into a working checklist for more systematic analysis. It then challenges them to take on the physicality of someone else through carefully observed imitation. It finally offers a complete physical warm-up, with suggestions for adapting preparation for a variety of circumstances.

Chapter 2 Healing Your Body

Understanding physical structure as a path for making mindful movement choices

This chapter takes the reader from a tentative acquaintance with the body's structure to a greatly expanded and detailed awareness. It offers guidance for developing a fitness/health regimen that prepares the actor for a range of challenges. Knowledge of physical anatomy helps lead to informed choices, prevention of misuse and greater performance control and power.

Chapter 3 Movement Masters

Examining the leading innovators and disciplines in actor movement training

Chapter 3 identifies the most prominent innovative contributors to movement education: Alexander, Bogart, Chekhov, Feldenkrais, Grotowski, Laban, Lecoq, Meyerhold, Stanislavski, Suzuki and Vakhtangov as well as the disciplines (Aikido, Alba Emoting, Chi Gung, Hakomi, Meditation, NLP, Reflexology, Rolfing, Shiatsu, T'ai chi, Visualization and Yoga) most widely practiced to aid actors in making informed choices for their own regimens.

Chapter 4 Evolving Movement

Developing a psychophysical vocabulary of movement methods suited to all theatre forms

This chapter focuses extensively on the movement master Rudolf Laban whose impact we feel has been particularly profound. It provides an opportunity for readers to expand their energy system and kinesthetic awareness through a focus on Laban's effort/shape and action categories. The use of images throughout expands physical imagination and the potential gestural language of a character, as well as the use of earth elements to increase awareness of dramatic principles of stage movement—*phrasing, transitions, intensity, stillness* and *development*. It also provides a method of observation and analysis for development of character studies.

Chapter 5 Character Creation

Exploring physical action in the development of a physical character

Chapter 5 provides you with the tools to assemble a character in a way that can integrate diverse venues, mediums and performance styles, from classical to realism to postmodernism. It assists you in generating internal images from which to enact a character and establish the center for your preparation for a role. This activation of your imagination to flush out all aspects of the character's internal and physical life provides the impetus to create physically and emotionally unique characters for the stage.

Chapter 6 Acting Spaces

Negotiating stage spaces for movement mastery

The core vocabulary for functioning in a theatre space and moving there is provided, the terms associated with theatre geography, along with tips for reading the map and navigating the areas, including a discussion of the relative strength of stage positions. Specific acting moves are identified, including changing locations, facial expressions, gestures or angling the body, some more and some less desirable, but all important to recognize. The impact of various stage compositions is explored in stillness and with the addition of motion. Differences in movement etiquette onstage and in daily life are examined. The tools for mastering self-staging are established, with emphasis on the use of the Circles of Concentration and the Method of Physical Actions to aid your focus and control.

Chapter 7 Acting Styles

Using information from the worlds of non-realistic plays to develop believable style characterizations

Chapter 7 tackles the challenge of transporting the audience and the actors themselves into another era, country, realm or imaginary universe. The most common of these are the ISMs, period styles, musical theatre and mix or fusion blends. Entering these worlds involves analyzing time, space, place, values, structure, beauty, sex, recreation, sight and sound represented in each play, along with considerable research. The similar characteristics shared by all classical roles are established as well as specific techniques unique to classical theatre.

Chapter 8 Movement Future

Continuing to grow as a performer

This chapter makes a strong case for meticulous research and experimentation into every dimension of the physical lives of all characters as an essential commitment for each actor's future. A considerable bibliography offers you a way into the study of all areas of movement independently. Categories for regular practice (aerobics, strength, flexibility, focus, coordination, composure and imagination) are suggested along with supplemental training in specialized, tangential movement disciplines. Guidelines for researching and choosing advanced training are offered.

While the text suggests a workable arc for expanding and deepening movement awareness, each chapter can function as a stand-alone if you prefer to explore topics that interest you in another sequence that simply satisfies your curiosity.

CHAPTER 1 BODY OWNERSHIP

Exercises:

Figures:

Class!

Homework

Everyone leads the warm up once?

Body Ownership

Analyzing individual movement histories and tendencies for deeper self-knowledge

You are your instrument. You need to know all about how your body works, your habits, your distinct ways of being. You need to know all about yourself before you can become someone else.

Angelina Jolie, actor

What You Already Know

In opening this book, you may be starting your movement training, but not your knowledge, which is already considerable. Unlike your voice, which is hiding inside a cave, your body *is* that cave and it is quite visible, so photos, video and mirrors have shown you your movement instrument. You may not know how to move like an older person, a Restoration dandy or a dancing fool, but you already have some idea how you navigate in the world. You know something about your height, weight, strength, motor skills, your waist and hat size, energy level, sleep needs and perhaps your body fat ratio, cardiovascular fitness, muscle tone and pain threshold. You have some qualitative sense of yourself as a dancer, athlete or mechanic. You know something about your habitual smile, frown or look of surprise. Our task will be to increase the range and sophistication of your body awareness, but take comfort in the fact that you are starting with knowledge that can be built upon.

The process we will pursue in this book is that followed by anyone who decides to make a change in her life and then succeeds. Someone who decides to get healthy focuses on the physical or the psychological self. Those who do well in fitness or therapy 1) start off gaining self-knowledge and acceptance, 2) move into correcting problems and then 3) work toward advanced skills and growth, constantly expanding their options. You are going to become an actor who uses her body better, onstage and off.

Begin by taking the time to recognize your own physical past. Feedback has shaped your self-concept, whether that feedback was accurate or not. Your physical history has been captured in photo albums, home videos and growth charts. It may even be represented by various boxes of clothing in the attic, but it is time to organize it in order to move forward.

EXERCISE 1.1 **MY BODY HISTORY**

1. EARLY FEEDBACK—Can you remember the first time anyone said anything to you about your movement? Was it being told to sit still, to hurry up, to stop fidgeting? How did you figure out which physical impulses would not necessarily be accepted? What positive feedback did you receive? What did you decide to try again because it seemed to go over well?
2. CONSISTENT FEEDBACK—What have been the most consistent responses to physical choices you have gotten over the years? Positive or negative, what has come up most often? Try closing your eyes and going back year-by-year through your life. It is valuable to bring back all the feedback received most frequently because some of it may have *really* left its mark.
3. TRYING TO CHANGE—Did you ever consciously try to change your body? When and why? Were you imitating or modeling yourself on someone else? What made you try? Did you succeed or give up? Did you try more than once?
4. INDIRECT FEEDBACK—Were there times when others didn't address your body or movement directly, but you *suspect* that was what got to them? Like being told not to be so hyper when you didn't feel hyper but must have seemed that way? Or being told to stop being serious when you thought you were just being neutral? When have you been misunderstood or misjudged because of your physical self rather than your real thoughts or behavior?
5. ACTING NOTES—If you've been involved with theatre for a while, what are your movement notes (from your director, teacher, coach, scene partner or even your family) most of the time? Be sure to establish both what you feel is good about your movement and what needs work.

The questions coming up in subsequent exercises are tough ones. All we ask is that you give your best possible conjecture, maybe even a guess. Your answers will get better every time you return and ask the questions.

EXERCISE 1.2 **MY MOVEMENT PROFILE**

Describe your body as if it has a personality or nature of its own. Come at it from the following angles:

1. EYE/AGILITY—Can you mimic others easily? Can you see something and re-create it? Are you facile with dance moves and good with sports, usually only having to be shown the maneuvers once? Was physical expression encouraged in your home?

Do you enjoy cutting loose outdoors or at parties? Or is that something you normally avoid or ignore?

2. CIRCUMSTANCES—How does your physical life change with your current state? Does your way of carrying yourself and contact with others alter depending on the kind of day you are having? Can others catch this? How radically and in what way?

3. MASKING—What tricks have you learned to cover up how you're really feeling? How do you try to conceal with your physical presentation? Are you good at being poker faced or covering up anger? Under what circumstances do you always give yourself away?

4. INFLUENCES—If you have a rural or big city background, can people tell that? Can they tell what *kind* of a place you came from even if they can't identify it?

5. HERITAGE—Does your family's past/history influence your movement? How do its national origins, race, religion, affiliations, cultural background or socio-economic class enter into the way you carry yourself? Do you control these influences?

6. CHRONOLOGY—How old are you? How old are you *physically*? Do you always get carded or conversely mistaken for someone more mature? Is your movement an accurate reflection of your chronological age? Of your spiritual age?

7. STRANGER ON FILM—When you see yourself on video, what surprises you? How are you different than what you expected? How does it violate or reinforce your self-concept?

8. AN ACTING BODY—Are you aware of differences from your private and even your public self, when you act? Not conscious *characterization* decisions, but rather unconscious alteration in your physical life when you hit the stage? Do you suddenly have trouble knowing what to do with your hands or conversely begin to gesture far more than in offstage life? How do you feel different?

Jot down the answers that seem to have validity. Be prepared to demonstrate in class how you are in each of the circumstances above. Trust yourself to sense which influences are strong.

The next step is to go back over your movement history and profile and confront what may be influencing you but should not. Was there behavior that was required in your upbringing that now tends to inhibit you in performance?

EXERCISE 1.3 TRACKING THE BLOCKS

1. STILL WITH ME—Make a list from the categories in Exercises 1.1 and 1.2 of those influences you feel are still strongly with you. If nothing comes to mind, you may want to start with a simple list of rewarded and punished behavior in your home, neighborhood, school or organizations of which you were a member and see where movement comes up.

2.   IN THE WAY—Decide which ones may be getting in your way. Circle them, remember them and be alert for the next situation in which you might want to stop and free yourself. We will be offering suggestions for achieving that freedom later in the chapter.
3.   OH, YEAH—Be alert for other influences that did not come up right away, but may pop into your memory now that the subject is there. Keep your list where you can add and review.

Note: Don't try to place blame. People who influenced you to move or not move one way or another probably had no idea you would want to be an actor someday and were mostly (even if ignorantly) trying to help you get on in life.

While sweeping the past, it is too easy to throw out everything, so take a moment to validate what is working and why. What has contributed to your physical strengths? Honor the parts of your movement tendencies that work for you.

EXERCISE 1.4 KEEPING THE GOOD STUFF

1.   STILL WITH ME—Make a list of positive influences still strongly with you.
2.   WANT THIS—Decide which ones you want to keep on board as a basis or firm structure for your future movement work. Circle them, remember them and be alert for the next situation in which you might want to stop and use what you know you have going for you.

Your Body Recipe

Time now to move beyond impressions to a more systematic analysis of your physical instrument. Public interest in the body, health, diet and exercise is at an all-time high. But as an actor you need to move beyond body as machine to body as interpretive instrument, understanding the choices you make and impressions you leave by just standing, sitting, walking or gesturing, as well as the impact of your own mannerisms. You must then understand how your tendencies may need adjustment depending on the role.

Your Body Recipe can consist of nine key ingredients:

1.   Standing
2.   Sitting
3.   Expression
4.   Tempo/Rhythm
5.   Motion
6.   Gestures

7. Adaptations
8. Cultural Binding
9. Mannerisms

For the following lists, observe how others use their bodies like or unlike you.

1. STANDING

   a. Where is your weight placed in your typical silhouette? Which part of your body really carries the load?
   b. Where are you centered? Does energy or drive radiate from one spot?
   c. How close to symmetrical are you? Do you lean or cross yourself or favor one side?
   d. What is your posture like? Do you slouch? Does it vary?
   e. Does any part of your body seem to dominate or draw focus?

2. SITTING

   a. How collapsed or erect are you when sitting? How much do you sink or release into the chair or floor?
   b. Do you lean? In what direction?
   c. Is your body crossed in one or more places? How tightly? Do you appear to be covering yourself anywhere? Are you sitting on any part of yourself, your own leg, a hand?
   d. How much space are you taking? Do you thrust out or exhibit any part of yourself? How open and expansive is the spread of your arms and legs?
   e. What curves are present? In the spine? The appendages? The tilt of the head? In more than one direction?

3. EXPRESSION

   a. What is the typical look you tend to have on your face? What are the three runners-up? What range of facial change do you habitually go through?
   b. Is your eye contact with others usually direct or not? How intense? How long before looking away? Do you squint, narrow your eyes, droop your lids or open your eyes wider?
   c. Any changes in other parts of the face? Do your eyebrows move? Do you wiggle your nose? Purse your lips? Suck in your cheeks?
   d. Do expressions generally linger or disappear abruptly? How are they timed? Does your smile come suddenly or slowly expand?
   e. Are you easy to read or are you somewhat "poker faced"? Are your expressions pronounced or subtle and muted? How lively and open is your face?

4. TEMPO/RHYTHM

   a. Are your movements fast, slow, medium? What is your basic rate?
   b. How constant is your tempo? Are you fairly predictable or do you change radically?
   c. Does your foot contact the ground with full weight or a glide, making only minimal contact with the ground? Are your steps heavy or light?

    d.   Do you punctuate or stress each move with any part of the body as you walk? Could someone tap your movement patterns like playing a drum?

    e.   What is the relationship between your speed and your rhythms? To what extent do they affect each other? Are you fast and erratic? Slow and steady? What combination?

5.   MOTION

    a.   When walking, sitting or leaning, where do you make contact with the surface below? Is the contact flat and solid or gradual and curved?

    b.   Do you prepare to move (shifting weight, adjusting clothing, swaying slightly) or do you just take off? When you stop, is there a recovery period of similar adjustments? Do you settle (even squirm) into stillness or just land and stop?

    c.   What kind of support do you give yourself? Do you reach out with your hands to furniture before you sit, lean on walls or corners as you round them, grab railings on stairways?

    d.   Is your pattern of movement fluid and effortless or jerky and labored? How obvious is the changing of gears as you accelerate or change direction?

    e.   Are the moves straight and assertive? Do you face your target directly and shoot for it or approach it indirectly? Do you ease into furniture sideways, sidle up to people, curve across a room, insinuate yourself into a space?

6.   GESTURES

    a.   Are your arm and hand movements expansive and wide? Or do you work tight to the torso and economically?

    b.   How frequently do you gesture? Can you sit on your hands without going crazy with the need to use them? Or are your gestures occasional and selective?

    c.   Do you have predictable and repetitive moves? Are they shared by many, or are they unique to you? Do you have props you always seem to be playing with?

    d.   Do you literally demonstrate your feelings/experience physically? Could someone who doesn't speak English figure out what you are saying because of this? Or are your hands more likely to move in abstract, less literal ways?

    e.   Are your shoulders engaged, do you lean in to make points, does the head join in? How connected are your gestures to the torso? How free or independent are they from the rest?

7.   ADAPTATIONS

The categories above cover times when there may be no particular stimuli for change. When you add stress or stimuli to an otherwise average day, how does your body respond? Alone or in a group, as you're touching someone or being touched, as your mood changes? How do you adjust to "space invasions"? You have an amount of space that you like to keep between you and others, an invisible bubble around you. It may be larger or smaller (or more or less flexible) than someone else's bubble. If you're on a mountaintop or in a crowded elevator, your bubble adjusts in size because you know what to expect. But your bubble bursts, and you're unhinged, when someone unexpectedly invades what you regard as personal space.

Some people respond with genuine horror to the most accidental "space invasions" of their bubble, forgetting that it's invisible. Others are mindless invaders, forgetting that just because they like bear hugs and pats on the fanny doesn't mean everyone they meet craves that kind of contact.

You can invade another's space by moving very close without touching (as in certain South American cultures, where people like only three or four inches between them for conversation), by enveloping, trapping, grabbing hold, gentle touching in an area the recipient considers off limits or by simply staring so that your eyes invade. Omitting overtly violent or sexual moves (in our culture, someone three or four inches away may intend one or both), there are still a wide range of invasions. We all have covert limits.

Identify how you react when external elements change, as in:

a. Public versus Private Behavior:

   Do you react differently in groups? When the focus of a large number of people turns to you? Do you find yourself shifting posture, relating to furniture in a different way, walking more or less lightly, changing your timing? Are you one of those people who only really come alive when there is an audience?

b. Space Invasions (Initiating and Receiving):

   What if actual physical contact with others is involved? Are you more likely to be an invader or a receiver? Do you initiate physical contact? What is your own desired distance? How unsettled are you when others close in? Do you adapt well? Are you more likely to touch a particular place on another person?

c. Mood Shifts (Up and Down):

   To what extent does your physical life express your emotional one? Is the receipt of good or bad news likely to show in your body language? Does the kind of day you're having affect your posture, eye contact and freedom of gestures? Does intense feeling explode into movement? Or do you mask shifts in feelings?

8. CULTURAL BINDING

Any group whose members share the same behavior is a *culture*. Behavioral scientists call it *binding* when you're tied so strongly to the group that you have trouble breaking away from group limitations, even when you need to. You can be bound emotionally but also by geography, conditioning, age, sex, family and personal interests. Binding is a problem when you want to be believably cast as a member of another group.

Try to identify these influences on your physical life:

a. Geography: Does everyone guess where you were born even if they don't hear you speak? Do people know you are from the city or the country without having to ask?
b. Family: Do you share a set of moves with your parents, siblings and other relatives?
c. Conditioning: Do you send information that you have been told for years not to assert

yourself in groups, lest you be thought overbearing? Or to push, shove, shout, grab attention, whatever it takes to get what you deserve? How evident is the rewarded behavior and the punished behavior that was part of your home, school or church?

d.   Interests: Can others tell your special skills and favorite activities? That you are a dancer, athlete, pianist, body builder, scholar?

e.   Age: Do people get your age right or wrong, and can this be because of how you carry yourself?

f.   Sex: On a scale of extreme sexual stereotypes, where are you? Do you fall into a traditional masculine/feminine image? An androgynous mix? Neutral or ambiguous? How flexible and changeable are you?

9.   MANNERISMS

When you are in no particular mood, personal tendencies are habitual, happening without thought or effort, automatically. From foot tapping to knuckle cracking to teeth grinding to shoulder shrugging, an isolated movement may be a response to stress or it may just be an unconscious, acquired taste. Some heads may lean sharply on every key word spoken ("chicken neck"); others tilt to one side when listening, toss hair back suddenly, nod repeatedly or sink down so far in the torso that the neck almost disappears. And this is just the start of a head list. You may need to actively solicit feedback from friends about any tendencies you have that clearly define you in contrast to others, may sometimes be distracting and would be the first items chosen for someone trying to imitate you.

EXERCISE 1.5 MAKING YOUR LIST, CHECKING IT TWICE

Go through each of the categories above, making notes with brief answers in either the spaces below or on a separate sheet of paper. Try to come up with at least a good guess. Place question marks after answers about which you are not quite sure.

Body Awareness Checklist

Note: These terms are all employed in the analyses on the preceding pages. If it is not immediately clear what the word means, review how it first appears, to help clarify its use in identifying your own tendencies.

Standing	**Sitting**	**Expression**
Center_____	Leaning_____	Contact_____
Carriage_____	Release_____	Typical_____
Symmetry_____	Crossing_____	Parts_____
Posture_____	Space_____	Timing_____
Focus_____	Curves_____	Clarity_____

Tempo/Rhythm _____	Motion _____	Gestures_____
Rate _____	Contact _____	Expansiveness_____
Changes_____	Prep./Recovery_____	Frequency _____
Weight _____	Support _____	Predictability _____
Punctuation _____	Pattern _____	Demonstration_____
Relationship_____	Assertiveness_____	Connection_____

Adaptations

Groups _____	Contact _____	Mood_____
Public Behavior_____	Receiving Invasion_____	Up _____
Private Behavior _____	Initiating Invasion _____	Down _____

Cultural Binding

Geography_____	Family _____	Conditioning_____
Interests_____	Age_____	Sex _____

Mannerisms

Head _____	Face _____	Torso _____

Physical Life Project

One of the best ways to master physical lives is to capture someone else's. If you are work-ing alone, you might imitate a good friend or someone you see on the street every day. If you are in a class, randomly select the name of a classmate (possibly two) and work on capturing the physical lives of these people, observing them in as many different contexts as possible: in groups, alone, one to one, calm, excited. Keep this a secret from your subject in order for the observation to be unobtrusive and for the subject to not get self-conscious around you.

uta First exersise

EXERCISE 1.6 **IMITATION**

Prepare a silent scenario (realistic behavior but with the sound turned off) which includes the following ingredients. As this other actor you:

1. Enter the classroom, interact with classmates, take some time deciding where to sit, change your mind and move somewhere else.

2.   Deal with getting your stuff (outer clothing, backpack/book bag, purse, etc.) settled, getting out something with which to take notes, and jot something down.
3.   Ask a question of the teacher and interact with her in some way.
4.   Volunteer to demonstrate something or to do a brief presentation. (The class may agree on a topic or it may be that something appropriate has already been done in class).
5.   React to receiving applause for your efforts and return to your seat.

(If you have drawn more than one name, your teacher will after some time reveal the name of the other student who is spying on the same person you are. Meet your partner and compare notes. Begin working together, checking in with each other daily, alerting each other to new developments in the case. At some point, decide which of you is going to be the Primary Presenter, who will be the first one up to demonstrate what he has discovered).

On the day the assignment is due

1.   If there are two presenters, start with the main imitation, then have the second imitator add or refine the presentation based on other insights.
2.   After about five presentations, have the imitators and those being imitated meet for a few minutes to handle questions and clarifications.

Without question, the work on yourself and on a classmate in this chapter will greatly expand your knowledge and choices, both onstage and off. You will have a far more detailed and layered sense of options in how you present yourself in the world and in the ways you can build a character. However, these tools are only as useful as your confidence in using them. We will now move to considering the two states, pressure and fear, that can inhibit actors from experiencing freedom and adventurous exploration. Once we identify the characteristics of pressure and fear, we will offer numerous ways to overcome them to become a playful and confident performer.

Pressure and Fear

In a recent large scale survey, fear of performing in public was the number one item chosen, even ironically surpassing death! Many are not able to gather the courage to give a short speech, much less take an acting course, much less audition for a play and certainly not face an audience of hundreds of potentially critical observers on opening night.

Because you are reading this, you are not among those who are overwhelmed. Yet the very nature of the pressures of performance and the ever looming disease of stage fright make it essential to counteract impulses which can sabotage even the most capable performers. So it is essential to identify the characteristics of pressure and fear and then to learn, through effective warm-ups, both physical and psychological, to keep them at bay and even to transcend them, achieving performance freedom.

In the rest of this book, we will offer you ways to calm down and get focused. We will give you detailed information about how your body structure works (Chapter 2) so that you can immediately recognize and head off symptoms as well as achieve productive wellness. We will familiarize you with numerous disciplines and the works of many movement masters (Chapter 3) to help you pick the regimens which will be most satisfying for you. We will provide you with ways to expand what your body knows and can do (Chapter 4), as well as paths to so thoroughly become a character (Chapter 5) that the last thing on your mind will be the pressure of performance or the fear of being judged. Rather you will be filled with calm focus and the joy of performing. You will experience a mastery of stage mechanics (Chapter 6) that will allow you to comfortably inhabit the stage and confidently explore it in character. Your character knowledge will expand to include periods and styles other than your own (Chapter 7) and beyond contemporary realism. We will also suggest some paths for continuing your lifelong journey (Chapter 8) of further movement mastery. You will move well beyond pressure and fear into power.

But first let's identify exactly what happens to you physically when you experience these emotional states.

How do these two conditions relate, compare and contrast? Pressure (or anxiety, tension, burden, strain, stress, frustration) is usually of far lighter immediate impact, but it lasts longer. Some of us have ongoing constant pressure in our work and/or living situations. While often manageable for a time, over the long haul cumulative effects can be devastating. Fear (or dread, wariness, alarm, fright, trepidation, terror) has far greater immediate impact, but it is usually of shorter duration, as it may be quickly resolved by the traditional flight or fight choice of action or a change in circumstances, such as finding out that the signals were false or exaggerated or that the danger has passed.

Knowledge of the specific details of both will not only aid you in countering them in life, but when as an actor you are asked to play these states, you will have a range of choices. Because drama is conflict, characters often experience both pressure and fear, yet you as an actor need to believably portray them in a skillful way without succumbing to the primary states themselves and thus losing control of your performance. These lists will help you put together a detailed performance that will still allow you mastery and authority in presentation.

In offstage life, you may need to change circumstances (a different job, a different roommate) to avoid omnipresent influences. In the theatre, you are likely to feel rehearsal pressure to produce results, to master what is asked of you quickly, such tasks as learning blocking and memorizing lines, to experiment, to find imaginative solutions toward achieving your performance. Fear may invade when you feel unprepared and not ready for scrutiny, for more than a few actors on opening night. In the life of the actor, fear is never more threatening than in an audition where you are potentially profoundly vulnerable and subject to rejection. The solution is not to focus on avoiding pressure and fear, but rather to place your focus elsewhere on your strength, calm, focus, clarity and joy. A primary tool in this shift is warming up, outlined later in this chapter.

STRESS AFFECTS EVERY CELL IN YOUR BODY.
THIS IS WHAT HAPPENS IF YOU DON'T CONTROL IT.

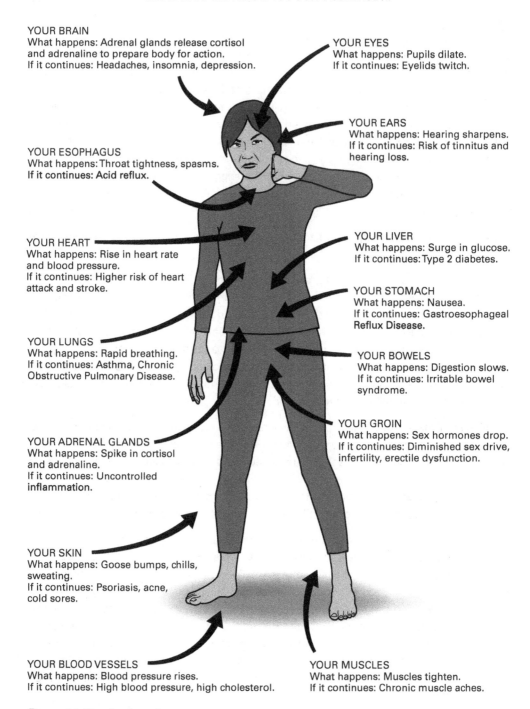

YOUR BRAIN
What happens: Adrenal glands release cortisol and adrenaline to prepare body for action.
If it continues: Headaches, insomnia, depression.

YOUR EYES
What happens: Pupils dilate.
If it continues: Eyelids twitch.

YOUR EARS
What happens: Hearing sharpens.
If it continues: Risk of tinnitus and hearing loss.

YOUR ESOPHAGUS
What happens: Throat tightness, spasms.
If it continues: Acid reflux.

YOUR HEART
What happens: Rise in heart rate and blood pressure.
If it continues: Higher risk of heart attack and stroke.

YOUR LIVER
What happens: Surge in glucose.
If it continues: Type 2 diabetes.

YOUR STOMACH
What happens: Nausea.
If it continues: Gastroesophageal Reflux Disease.

YOUR LUNGS
What happens: Rapid breathing.
If it continues: Asthma, Chronic Obstructive Pulmonary Disease.

YOUR BOWELS
What happens: Digestion slows.
If it continues: Irritable bowel syndrome.

YOUR GROIN
What happens: Sex hormones drop.
If it continues: Diminished sex drive, infertility, erectile dysfunction.

YOUR ADRENAL GLANDS
What happens: Spike in cortisol and adrenaline.
If it continues: Uncontrolled inflammation.

YOUR SKIN
What happens: Goose bumps, chills, sweating.
If it continues: Psoriasis, acne, cold sores.

YOUR BLOOD VESSELS
What happens: Blood pressure rises.
If it continues: High blood pressure, high cholesterol.

YOUR MUSCLES
What happens: Muscles tighten.
If it continues: Chronic muscle aches.

Figure 1.1 Your body under pressure

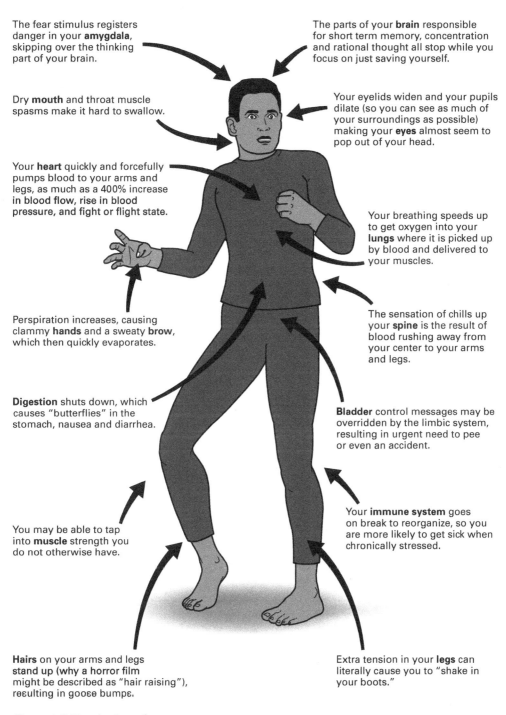

The fear stimulus registers danger in your **amygdala**, skipping over the thinking part of your brain.

The parts of your **brain** responsible for short term memory, concentration and rational thought all stop while you focus on just saving yourself.

Dry **mouth** and throat muscle spasms make it hard to swallow.

Your eyelids widen and your pupils dilate (so you can see as much of your surroundings as possible) making your **eyes** almost seem to pop out of your head.

Your **heart** quickly and forcefully pumps blood to your arms and legs, as much as a 400% increase in blood flow, rise in blood pressure, and fight or flight state.

Your breathing speeds up to get oxygen into your **lungs** where it is picked up by blood and delivered to your muscles.

Perspiration increases, causing clammy **hands** and a sweaty **brow**, which then quickly evaporates.

The sensation of chills up your **spine** is the result of blood rushing away from your center to your arms and legs.

Digestion shuts down, which causes "butterflies" in the stomach, nausea and diarrhea.

Bladder control messages may be overridden by the limbic system, resulting in urgent need to pee or even an accident.

You may be able to tap into **muscle** strength you do not otherwise have.

Your **immune system** goes on break to reorganize, so you are more likely to get sick when chronically stressed.

Hairs on your arms and legs stand up (why a horror film might be described as "hair raising"), resulting in goose bumps.

Extra tension in your **legs** can literally cause you to "shake in your boots."

Figure 1.2 Your body on fear

in class ?

EXERCISE 1.7 **YOUR OWN PRESSURE/FEAR ANALYSIS**

1. When you experience PRESSURE, which of the 14 characteristics listed above of ways it manifests itself in the body is likely to appear first? Which is likely to dominate?
2. Which are the least likely manifestations for you personally?
3. Under PRESSURE, how do your nine Body Recipe ingredients (see p. 4) change? What adaptations (#7) do you make?
4. Do you have strategies for concealing the pressure you are feeling?
5. Answer questions 1–4 for when you are experiencing FEAR?
6. How are you similar to or entirely different from the person you are imitating in these circumstances?

Applying Body Awareness

What do you do with this information now? It depends on how close or distant your "mirror" was to what you'd expected. How pleased or distressed are you by what has just been reflected to you? Do any of your mannerisms interfere with the effectiveness of your communication? What you communicate may be just fine, and you now have self-awareness to add to self-acceptance. Or you may choose to proceed with some changes. If you want to change, you can apply skills you developed in imitating others. Also, any of the details observed in other actors can be compiled and used when you wish to create a characterization that is different from your standard behavior. You are on your way to having more physical choices in any circumstance, onstage or off.

Warming Up

The ideal state for performing is relaxed readiness. Too *relaxed*, you fall asleep. Too *ready!*, you can explode, so actors seek a balance between ease and eagerness. While learning the following sequence, keep yourself open and responsive. Rituals of preparation vary widely, but the following sequence of activities is that most commonly used:

Figure 1.3 Breathing. Copyright the Cartoonist Group.

1. Breathing
2. Meditation
3. Tensing/Releasing
4. Alignment
5. Shaking
6. Stretching
7. Energizing
8. Aerobics

Modify any exercise if it appears to give you strain today. Drop out if you don't feel well. No need to explain your decision if you are working in a group. Just fade subtly out until you feel you can rejoin. Breathe fully throughout each exercise. Guidelines will be provided, but it is most important to just let each breath move you along, and help you loosen up.

1. BREATHING

A warm-up is most effective if it starts with breath. We will begin with basic deep breathing as most of us habitually breathe in a way that is far too shallow. Read through the steps below before performing the exercise, as the stages follow each other rapidly, almost overlapping.

Consciously record air passing through each of the following areas.

- *Nose and throat:* Deeply inhale, primarily through the nose while allowing the mouth to open slightly.
- *Upper chest:* Let air pass through without any expansion in this area.
- *Floating ribs:* Feel them open like a double door of welcome for the air. The three sets of lower ribs (unlike the others) are unattached at the front, so when they part, air flows fully.
- *Diaphragm:* Normally in a double arched and raised position it both lowers and flattens as deep breathing occurs. Feel your lower torso expand to its fullest as the diaphragm descends.
- *Lower back:* Finally, experience the air reaching deeply into this most efficient, often unused, storage room.

Now sigh out in exhalation, mouth fully open, allowing sound, recording the reversal of the process, as the air moves out and past:

- lower back
- diaphragm
- floating ribs
- upper chest
- mouth

Particularly if you are accustomed to "sucking in" your stomach area, it is vital that you do the opposite when inhaling. You should feel expansion all around your entire middle as if you have a tire that encircles you. Conversely, as you allow exhalation, allow a mild contraction of your abdominal muscles as you empty that area. So you should feel "fattest" at the end of inhalation and "thinnest" at the end of exhalation.

Unless otherwise indicated, this basic breathing pattern is one to maintain throughout the exercises that follow. Breathing guidelines will be provided at the side of each exercise.

2.   MEDITATION

Meditation is usually done sitting or lying on the floor and involves the repetition of a sound silently to yourself.

(Breathing: Start with deep breaths and then allow them to become ever more shallow as you go deeper into the meditative state and concentration turns inward.)

Here and Now, Part I

1.   Let go of the past and the future. Like heavy, cumbersome layers of clothing, let them drop aside. Be in no time or place but right in this moment, in this room, either alone or surrounded by other actor friends. Let the earlier part of the day, and the later part still ahead, drift away, so you feel completely here, now.
2.   Pick out small physical sensations: jewelry against your skin, places clothes feel loose or tight, a radiator humming, your own shallow breathing, the places your body makes contact with the floor—anything too tiny or trivial to normally notice.
3.   Choose a word or sound that pleases you: a suggestive verb, such as *soothe, ease, release, complete, renew,* or something purely sensual and abstract, such as *velvet, music, embrace* or *dawn,* the name of a favorite object, place, or a nonsense syllable that makes you feel good. Repeat the word silently to yourself, continuously, without any effort, letting the qualities of the word wash over you and allowing your mind to wander where it will.

The time devoted will vary depending on the needs of the group. If everyone seems high strung today, it may be extended. If there is a sense of calm unity already in the room, even two minutes may be enough.

3.   TENSING/RELEASING

Adding some tension to an area of the body just before letting that area unwind or fall free almost always leads to greater release. A moderately tensed muscle relaxes more when let go than it would from a neutral state, and the immediate contrast can produce a pleasurable, easy feeling.

The Prune

(Breathing: Breathe in deeply before doing this exercise. Then hold your breath as long as you can while going through your tensing body inventory. And once you have fully tensed, let the exhalation fully release as you relax.)

1. Lie on your back with arms and legs uncrossed and loose. As each area of the body is called, tense it up, keeping everything lower on your body loose and relaxed. The tension will accumulate, moving from head to toes, before you finally let everything go and float from the release.
2. First, tense all your facial muscles inward toward the center of the face, as if it were rapidly withering and drying up into a prune.
3. Tighten the surrounding skull as if it were suddenly locked in a vice.
4. Shoot the tension into the neck as if it were in a brace and frozen in place.
5. Shoot it across the shoulders, locking at the shoulder joints. (Remember that everything below the shoulders is still loose.)
6. Tighten the upper arms, both sets of biceps and triceps.
7. Tense at the elbows, locking the elbow joints,
8. into the lower arms,
9. locking the wrists as if they were tightly bound,
10. tightening the palms of the hands as if catching a ball,
11. drawing the fingers halfway into a fist that will not complete itself but remains suspended and part-closed.
12. Tighten upper chest and back,
13. stomach and lower back as if protecting against a blow.
14. Tense hip joints, which are then locked.
15. Tense the groin area and the buttocks,
16. stiffen upper legs,
17. lock the knee joints,
18. draw lower legs taut,
19. lock ankles,
20. stiffen feet, extending toes.
21. Point toes finally at the wall opposite you.
22. Final position: Pull upward toward the ceiling at the center of your body, so that your torso is lifted up off the ground and your body is supported only by the back of the head, the shoulder blades and your heels, as if the whole body were drying up like a prune. Hold, then
23. release, letting it all go, feeling almost as if you're sinking into the floor or floating in the air but in no way confined anymore by gravity. Relax and savor the sensation of easy, released floating.
24. Repeat more quickly, remembering to keep everything loose until it is called: Tighten face, head, neck, shoulders, upper arms, elbows, lower arms, wrists, hands, fingers halfway into fist, upper chest and back, stomach and lower back, hip joints, groin and buttocks, upper legs, knee joints, lowers legs, ankles, feet, toes pointed, body pulled up toward ceiling and release. And savor.

4. ALIGNMENT

The spinal column is a primary center for the body. Vertebrae can close off to shorten the spine, thereby blocking physical and emotional responsiveness. But the column can be returned to an open state by lying on the floor and allowing the space between each vertebra to return as the back stretches toward an aligned state and the rest of the body follows.

The Accordion

(Breathing: Let your breath feel easy and gentle. Imagine you inhale and exhale into and out all along your spinal column as you release each vertebra into total relaxation.)

1. Still on your back, and without pushing to achieve it, simply allow your spine to stretch out along the floor. Imagine your body is like thick syrup that has splashed on the floor and slowly, easily spreads in every direction.
2. The back should be absolutely flat against the floor. This feeling may be achieved more easily by slowly raising the knees and slightly extending the elbows to the side. Shift until you find your own flattest, easiest position.
3. Imagine the spine as a hand accordion stretching to its full length but still undulating gently and feeling no pressure, while you continue to inhale and exhale easily.
4. Imagine air whirling gently around each of the vertebrae as they all ease apart. Imagine that your head is several miles away from your tailbone as these two ease gently in opposite directions.
5. Roll over on your side into a curled position and slowly move to a standing position by uncoiling, with the head the very last part to reach the top and the column returning to the same aligned, stretched sensation that it had when pressed against the floor.
6. Now think of your head as a balloon floating high above the rest of the body, which hangs comfortably from the balloon. Plant your feet firmly and imagine them many, many miles away from your head-balloon. You should feel as if your posture is terrific but was achieved without effort and maintained without strain.
7. Sense your accordion-spine moving imperceptibly, comfortably stretching.

The Puppet

(Breathing: Inhale just before collapsing, then exhale as you do so. Breathe normally and effortlessly as you test your looseness.)

1. Drop the entire upper body forward like a puppet, bending at the waist so your hands almost brush the floor.
2. Let the knees bend slightly and then use the lower body only for balance and support, ignoring it otherwise and letting the entire upper body hang loose and limp.
3. Test your own looseness by swinging arms and head, apelike, back and forth.
4. Imagine a string connected to your tailbone that begins to tug you up toward the ceiling as if a puppeteer is pulling you into life. Imagine similar strings connected to each of the 30-plus vertebrae all the way up into the back of your skull.
5. Allow yourself to rise very slowly, string by string, untensing slightly with each tug. Avoid any temptation to pull upper back, neck and head up too early. They're the very last strings. You'll reach a completely erect position before your neck even begins to rise.
6. Collapse again and repeat.

5.   SHAKING

At any of the joints (wrists, elbows, shoulders and so on), stiffness or the false sensation of cramp in a nearby muscle may be relieved by spinning the appendage in a circle or just shaking it out. The sudden rush of activity tends to awaken that area of the body, so it joins the rest of you and takes part again.

Rag Doll

(Breathing: Let the air shoot out or in whatever pattern feels right.)

1.   Imagine yourself as loose as a rag doll or scarecrow and simply shake out, standing in place, wherever you feel a little tight.
2.   Spend some time on just the wrists, then elbows, then the whole arm from the shoulder joint, then alternating legs, and finally all of these going at random.

Return to shaking at any point in the exercise sequence when you feel like it. Don't isolate it at this point, but return to shaking regularly, as a constant way of loosening and filling time while you may be waiting for others to complete an exercise.

6.   STRETCHING

In physical conditioning, stretching is an effective counterbalance to a muscle-building activity. The muscles narrow and contract as they build, restricting flexibility, as in "muscle bound." Stretching gives pliability, adding grace to strength, keeping muscles supple and the body flexible. While animals seem to know instinctively how to stretch, humans have largely forgotten. The upper back and neck areas tend to gather tension and particularly benefit from stretching.

Head Rolls

(Breathing: Let your forward rolls be exhalation and then allow the upward turn to inhalation, effortlessly and gradually transitioning from air in to out.)

1.   Standing tall, with feet firmly planted, let your head drop forward into your chest, chin landing gently on your clavicle.
2.   Begin slowly rolling your head in either direction in a moderate circle that grows in size with each repetition, without ever having your head move more than ever so slightly to the back while allowing it to go more fully to each side and to the front. Your circle, no matter what its size, favors forward movement.
3.   Change directions after you work your way to a wide circle.
4.   Keep the rest of the body upright, and isolate the action to the head and neck, with shoulders and chest in no way active. Make no effort to keep your mouth closed or eyes shut, but let them drop if you feel the impulse. If you feel like lingering briefly at any point, go ahead. Sense where you need to linger. If you feel like it, increase the speed of the circles, but only if that feels good today.
5.   It may help to think of the neck as a ball bearing at the connection between torso and

head, a ball bearing firmly placed but capable of a large range of safe motion. (The only potentially unsafe action is in dropping the head backward.)

A stretched body is capable of reaching farther without strain. Physical stretching can make you feel more capable of emotional, creative stretching as well.

The Sun

This is one of many variations of a yoga-based exercise that stretches the whole body and can be infused with optional spiritual connotations as you worship the sun, salute it, or (if the day is overcast) try to will it into appearing.

There are 11 positions: 1 and 11 are the same. So are 2, 5, 7 and 10. This will be more complicated than anything we've done so far, but the stretch is worth it.

(Breathing: It will be tempting to hold your breath, so don't forget to breathe! After the initial asana, alternate the strong inhalation suggested in the first stage with regular considered exhalation, inhaling on the odd numbered and exhaling on the even numbered stages.)

1. Stand tall, hands clasped, palms together, as in prayer or traditional Asian greeting.
2. While inhaling, explode into a giant X figure, arms and legs wide and open, leaning back slightly to face the sun.
3. Pull your legs together and, keeping them straight, bend your upper body over (as in toe touches), with your hands grasping your ankles, getting full stretch along the back of the legs while exhaling. If you need to, allow your knees to bend slightly as you do so.
4. Spread your hands out on the floor, supporting your body (as at the beginning of a push-up) but with only one leg extended behind, while the other is bent beneath the upper body, stretching the extended side of the body while inhaling. The overall position is similar to a sprinter about to take off. (In each of these full body stretches, the head is tilted slightly back so that the line from head to foot is a very moderate C-shaped curve).
5. Extend the leg that was bent to join the other and, exhaling, move your body into an upside-down V, with your buttocks being the point of the V and high in the air.
6. Lower your upper body as if to do a push-up, but as your face nears the floor, curve your torso back into a cobra position, providing a gentle stretch along your lower back and upper legs, inhaling.
7. Repeat the upside-down V while exhaling.
8. Inhaling, repeat the stretch in position 4, reversing extended and bent legs so that the stretch is on the other side of the body.
9. Bring your feet together and, supporting your weight, curl your body into the smallest possible position (approximately fetal), head against knees and arms wrapped around lower legs. Squeeze yourself inward in preparation to explode out. Inhale, exhale and inhale again in this position.
10. Exhaling, repeat the X full salute of position 2.
11. Repeat the hands-clasped stillness of position 1.

Eventually, when all moves are second nature, perform the Sun as one continuous, flowing action. Pulse slightly in each location, but imagine a floating, unbroken, easy dance, with all moves having the fluid, spineless quality of the cobra for which position 6 is named.

Alternative: If time and space make it difficult to do the Sun, just take a few minutes to stretch anywhere you feel tight, working your way gradually through the body as a simple substitute.

7.   ENERGIZING

The term "breath support" means more than having enough air to speak. The following touches on the deepest breathing because most of us need to be reminded of the reserves of breath storage. Also, in this warm-up sequence, it's time for something truly invigorating.

Lung Vacuum

This exercise literally cleans out stale air and replaces it forcibly. Some dizziness is natural, particularly for smokers, at the very beginning.

(Breathing: Be unafraid to make noise, in fact be sure to do so, both when blowing out and adding the last few loud puffs and then when it comes rushing in with a loud receptive sucking sound.)

1.   Collapse exactly as in the Puppet, simultaneously blowing air out vigorously (and audibly) through the mouth.
2.   In the collapsed position, continue to blow out air in short, powerful spurts until you feel completely emptied. Imagine that you need to get rid of harmful fumes and replace them with clean air, but that it will only work if you are totally empty. Proceed at your own rate, with no need for group coordination.
3.   Rise slowly, keeping air out, making sure your footing is secure and solid. Keep it out as long as you can manage it.
4.   When you feel you must breathe, allow air to sweep in, feeling it pour almost to the end of your fingertips and toes. Notice the rush of air to the small of the back. You should feel an intense rush as the new air sucks in with a vacuum force.
5.   Repeat the sequence at your own rate.

Actors work to inhale faster (so they don't waste valuable time) and to exhale more slowly (so they can speak longer and more confidently). This exercise is an intensification of that sensation, with exhalation extended for quite a while and inhalation happening in an instant.

Note: The following two sequences should be considered optional. If the vocal warm-up is being included, it should be inserted at this point.

8.   AEROBICS

A regularly raised, sustained heartbeat makes for cardiovascular fitness and health fringe benefits. However, long-term benefits are not the reason for aerobic exercise in this warm-up, which is designed to get the heart pumping and the blood flowing after the calmer earlier activities.

(Breathing: In both of these sequences, simply remember to breathe deeply and never hold your breath. Try to establish an inhalation/exhalation pattern that is in sync rhythmically with the activities.)

The Blender

This sequence is performed as fast as the group can manage it and is usually done watching someone lead the movement. The leader calls moves with a definite, clear beat. Everyone bounces lightly on the balls of the feet throughout.

- *Two jumping jacks:* Familiar exercise with leader setting time.
- *Two elbows to knees:* Elbow touches opposite knee, as the other arm swings high in the air, then other elbow touches other knee.
- *Two touch feet in backs:* Hand-slap shoe in same opposition as step 2 (left hand to right foot, right hand to left foot) as foot is raised in back. Again, unused arm swings high in the air.
- *Two side jacks:* Same as jumping jacks, except body is turned sideways each time, with one arm to the front and the other back, one leg bent to one side, and the other leg straight and extended to the other side.
- *Two kicks:* One leg up and forward, with both arms extended out to the sides.
- *Two starbursts:* Similar to positions 2 and 10 in the Sun. Dip with hands just above knees and then leap off the ground into a big, open X in the air.

The Journey

Imagine that you're on a wild journey through various terrains and are being pursued by some monster or demon. Go through the following maneuvers, continuing to dip or jump up and down in a stationary position. Explore as a group how best to represent the activity while remaining in one spot:

- Swimming
- Climbing a ladder
- Skating
- Climbing a rope
- Riding a horse
- Slalom skiing
- Rowing a canoe
- Trying to fly

Finally, decide to stand up and assault the demon (as David did Goliath):

- Wind up your sling and then fire your victorious stone at the demon, jumping for joy as the monster crashes to the ground.

Alternative: Find a theme to keep everyone active and engaged for at least two minutes. Act out as many sports as possible with quick changes. Become as many different animals as you can in that time. Run outside and around the building and then back into the classroom—anything that gets the pulse up and charged.

Here and Now, Part II

(Breathing: As with the initial meditative sequence, start with deep breaths and then allow them to become ever more shallow as you go deeper into the meditative state.)

Return to a sitting or lying position, close your eyes and renew your sense of here and now, with the added stimuli of the preceding exercises. Drop away any lingering past or future distractions, touch on some immediate physical sensations, repeat a word or sound that makes you feel good. Allow yourself to feel a part of the group around you, comfortable and ready.

EXERCISE 1.8 BODY MEMORY

1. Make every effort to memorize the warm-up above completely, so that even if someone else is leading it, you know what is coming next.
2. Commit at least one exercise per day to memory. Use this list to test yourself. For the first workout, see if you can briefly define the concept. For those following, identify the sequence of events to complete each exercise:

   - Meditation (Here and Now 1 and 2)
   - Tensing/Releasing (The Prune)
   - Alignment (The Accordion, The Puppet)
   - Shaking (Rag Doll)
   - Stretching (Head Rolls, The Sun)
   - Breathing (Lung Vacuum)
   - Aerobics (The Blender, The Journey)

3. Be prepared to lead the entire warm-up at a rehearsal or class meeting, using minimal notes.
4. When you can practically do it in your sleep, you will find that the effectiveness of the sequence increases significantly. This is because none of your energy is going into trying to get the moves right and you can now totally accept what the exercises have to offer you.

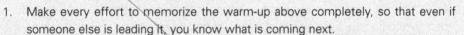

Changing Images

Countless exercises could be substituted for any of the above. But you don't want new exercises every day. If you keep changing warm-ups, you rarely master any. Your energy is too focused on learning the next move. If you're bored with a warm-up, it's because you're not yet giving yourself up to it, able to do it mindlessly, without struggling to remember what's next, thereby freeing your mind, moving beyond boredom to transcendence. The variety and enhancement can come with the *images* you change in your head. And you have great freedom to explore various images because you no longer need to concentrate on the warm-up activities which now come naturally.

Here are some possibilities:

- *Prune:* You age radically with each tensing. You're a hideous crone (like *The Picture of Dorian Gray*) by the last "pruning." Youth and vigor all return as you release. You are rejuvenated and renewed.
- *Accordion:* As your spine lengthens, so do you. You are Gulliver being tugged at gently by the Lilliputians or Paul Bunyan napping luxuriously over acres of timberland. When you stand, you can see across continents.
- *Head Rolls:* You are Samson or Rapunzel. You have an amazing mane of hair that whirls in slow motion around you like a cloud. Each roll of the head increases your own power, beauty, pride in your mane.
- *Puppet:* You're an ape when you collapse. At each tug along the spine, you move through an evolutionary cycle from primitive to a fully formed human of the future (passing through Oog about one-third of the way up), bright, complete and ready to conquer new worlds.
- *Sun:* You are a much-revered priestess or medicine man. Your people have pinned all their hopes for survival on you. Each move is a supplication to nature for spring to arrive and save your people from the cold. You literally will the sun to come out and warm those under your care.
- *Lung Vacuum:* You are saving the world. At great peril to yourself, you have breathed in toxic fumes, which you now blow out of your body and off the planet. You are successful and when you inhale, you are cleansed and safe.
- *Blender:* It is an Olympics far into the future, and you have been chosen the healthiest and most beautiful human in the world. You are dancing for a throng of people who wish to emulate you. Each move has them gasping with wonder. Each move fills you with power, which those who watch share because your energy is contagious.

It helps warm up the mind if physical maneuvers are accompanied by a rigorous workout of the imagination. You might pick a theme for a given session (the examples given are all about *power* and *heroism*) depending on your interests or needs that day. If you are warming up for a character, you might direct images to the character's background/perspective so you are entering her world through each exercise.

When and Where to Warm Up

A group warm-up may open a class, rehearsal or preparation for a performance. Or not. If you are preparing to perform and this is not offered, allow yourself time to warm up independently.

Edit, vary or expand an exercise according to the occasion and your own needs. If you antici-pate pressure or fear, prepare by warming up in advance. If you find you really need to stretch and meditate, but are less in need of aerobic stimulation, adapt or customize for yourself.

If a group warm-up is conducted, feel free to cut back or drop out of any activity depending on how you are doing today. You may feel stiff or under the weather or simply fragile. Trust your inner wisdom to guide what you can do full out and where you need to modify. No need to explain. Just remove yourself as unobtrusively as possible.

For warming up independently, adapt to your immediate circumstances. If you're in a crowded room, a quick Prune isn't possible, physically or emotionally. If you've only got two minutes, a complete here and now can't be done. But you can tense and release along the spine and both sides of the torso, even sitting in a chair, if you work with modifications. And you can think of soothing images, focus on something in this strange room that isn't strange but is instead comforting. You can repeat a sound that settles you, even for just a few moments. The secret of warm-ups is in adapting them, but not neglecting them.

Offstage Adaptations

Every situation you encounter in the theatre has some parallel outside. Every activity in this chapter has potential offstage use. In particular, use your Body Awareness when encountering new people, noting areas where your physical decisions have been misinterpreted by others and modifying accordingly to leave a more accurate impression. Find times in any day when a given activity may enhance your experience. The Prune is a great muscle relaxer if you are having trouble sleeping (and if we didn't move immediately on in class, many actors would doze off). A here and now may help you enjoy a family reunion and stop you dwelling on the fight you had with your girlfriend or boyfriend before vacation, and the paper that will be due (but you know you won't write until) the week after next. It may help you be with your family, so you don't miss the moment. Actors are hardly the only people tempted to get so caught up in their pasts and futures that they seem to overlook their presents altogether.

Summary

You already have knowledge of how your body works and past influences on your movement tendencies. Answering questions about your history and feedback you have received can now bring these influences into active consciousness. Putting together your own Body Recipe with nine crucial ingredients helps give shape and organization to your self-awareness and clarifies where work should be done. Observing yourself and partner, responding to a variety of circumstances, will now give you tools for both heading off those that are unwanted and details to use in building a basic character. You now hopefully have a true sense of ownership regarding your body. A thorough physical warm-up offers you the chance to effectively prepare for any performance challenge and helps you adapt to circumstances in and out of the theatre.

CHAPTER 2 HEALING YOUR BODY

Healing Your Body

Understanding physical structure as
a path for making mindful movement
choices

*I know that when I feel strong and my back is the source of strength, I feel the earth
beneath my feet. I feel something going right up through me, very strong, clean and
washed all the way through. It is of the utmost importance for one's body to be so
obedient to the impulses that come, that they obey you.*

Vanessa Redgrave, actor

Attention is built in many layers and they do not interfere with one another.
Constantin Stanislavski, acting teacher and theorist

You do not have to be ill to heal, the term which evolved from the word "whole," as in
harmonious, free from defect, balanced and fully integrated. We now move from the basic
self-awareness of the last chapter to a more complete understanding of how your body works
and how it might work better. Having established that you know quite a bit about your own
instrument, it is time to identify what you need to fill in the gaps to know and grow more.

An Actor Athlete

A concert pianist works with a keyboard, a mechanic with an engine, a painter with a canvas.
As an actor you work with yourself. You *are* your keyboard, engine and canvas. You are both the
artist and the vessel of the art. Even though you may be working with a playwright's ideas, the
script is no longer present at the moment of performance. There you are. Just you. This can be
frightening and yet fulfilling. It can be frustrating when you cannot stand back and examine your
art because you are it. It can be thrilling when you feel your art permeating your entire being.

To be the best actor possible you will want to strive to reach an "actor athlete" level of fitness.
You may not have any discernible athletic skills and that is OK. You just want to be as tuned
and healthy as an athlete, so your body never gets in your way and in fact opens the way to
acting possibilities.

There are successful actors who lead lives of decadence and indulgence, but if they have made it that far, they probably possess genius and survive/thrive in *spite* of their lifestyle choices. For the rest of us, it is essential to be in the best possible shape, with a body responsive to countless acting physical demands. Quite simply, your chances for success are far greater with the best possible working body.

Warming Up vs. Working Out

You warm up to prepare to participate in a specific event. As an actor, this is usually an audition, a class, a rehearsal or a performance. Outside the theatre, it may also be a particular athletic event or a challenging personal encounter. You warm up what you will need, the specific physical and emotional muscles that are likely to be engaged and which you do not wish to strain or damage by the effort involved.

You work out to improve and then maintain an overall level of fitness. Work outs often focus on cardiovascular work, muscle tone, flexibility or endurance. They are usually more general and are done daily or at least frequently on a schedule. They aim not to prepare you for a finite event, but to help you with your ongoing readiness to take on life's challenges in a healthy and energized way.

Fitness Focus

It is beyond the scope of this book to create physical fitness programs for our readers. Besides, you will want to find one (or design one) that entirely suits you. Let there be no doubt, however, that a fit actor moves better. If you have already found a program that works for you, good for you. If not, turn to Appendix A Finding Fitness for some motivation, some major categories and some tips to consider in pursuing a fitness program.

An activity that is being integrated by more and more people into their workout time is yoga. It is a physical discipline that integrates stretching and strengthening, through breath and physical positions that combine lengthening muscles with strengthening them. Muscle groups enriched in this way are generally longer in shape and form, giving a longer look to the body silhouette than muscles built primarily through the effort of such activities as weight lifting.

One of the primary gauges of fitness is aerobic endurance, a function of how well and how efficiently you use oxygen. To determine your level of endurance you need information from three heart rates: resting, working and recovery, as well as perceived level of exertion and an understanding of your own capacity. Turn to Appendix B Heart Rates for information on gauging these elements of aerobic endurance.

Whether you are warming up or working out, it is important to maintain consistent discipline. Stephen Covey, the author of the *Seven Habits* series, removes the authoritarian overtones from the term discipline and redefines it to mean "becoming the disciple of your own life." Personal discipleship means you care for your entire being: the food and substances you put in your body, the images you integrate into your imagination, the time you give to your physical development, and the balance you develop between commitment to your craft and the supportive environment of friends and family. The following list of questions is not to elicit a critique of yourself. As with the inventory in Chapter 1, it is an opportunity to consider what you are currently doing and what changes you want to implement.

EXERCISE 2.1 **SELF-INVENTORY**

1. Do you smoke? Do you work or live in a smoky environment?
2. Do you take any medications for treatment of an ongoing illness?
3. What is your height and weight? How do you feel about the latter?
4. What is the basis for your daily diet? Carnivore? Vegetarian?
5. How much water do you include as part of your daily intake?
6. What is your physical regimen? What does it include in terms of daily/weekly meditation/contemplation, stretch/flexibility, strength building and aerobics?
7. Which part of this regimen do you feel most attuned to? What is your assessment of your focus, flexibility, strength and aerobic fitness?
8. What is your felt sense of your alignment between your head, spine, hips, knees, ankles and feet?
9. What images of the ideal body are part of your conception of self? Do they come from family or friends? Stories you were read as a child? The media as in advertising, television, film or internet?
10. Rate your relative degree of satisfaction or contentment with each of your answers above on a scale of 1 to 10. For those under 5, at least consider that while you are studying and applying movement onstage and off might be a good time to instigate some changes.

Being aware of your current state allows you to respond more directly and effectively. For example, knowing where you are stiff allows you to engage in exercises that will develop flexibility. Embrace the opportunities offered here and you may be surprised by what else you have allowed to happen in terms of growth. If you consistently return to being the "disciple" of your life, you engage in a dialogue with yourself that will welcome, accept and embrace the experiences and states of the moment while assimilating new ways of being:

> To learn we need time, attention, and discrimination; to discriminate we must sense. In order to learn we must sharpen our powers of sensing, and if we try to do most things by sheer force we shall achieve precisely the opposite of what we need.
> **Moshe Feldenkrais, founder of the Feldenkrais Method of Somatic Education**

As you pursue each of the explorations that follow, allow yourself a three-part process:

1. You will want to place yourself in a state of "the first time"—a mode of inquiry, investigation and search.

2. You will want to note new levels of awareness, asking "What do I know about myself I did not know before?"

3. As you apply the new information, avoid placing judgment on the quality of the experience. Acknowledge all thoughts as information and then return to exploring the exercise. Allow yourself to develop a new set of voices that nurture your development. Open yourself to the possibilities offered by just saying "yes."

The following exercise is a step in the process of increased awareness. Once this awareness has been developed, it can be applied to virtually all physical activities. It will help you begin to feel the entirety, internally and externally, of your presence. As awareness increases, you will notice subtle shifts in the quality and intensity of your movement. The body scan exercise can be used at the beginning of all working sessions.

EXERCISE 2.2 BODY SCANNING

During the following, thoughts may arise that try to take the focus away from your objective. Without judging yourself or the thoughts, allow them to dissolve as if they were theatrical smoke dissipating with the development of the play's action and bring yourself back to the exercise.

1. Begin by lying on the floor on your back, feet long and arms at your side, with your eyes closed.

2. Starting either from your feet or head, investigate the external aspects of yourself. Note your relationship to the floor. What parts of you are released into the floor and what parts are not? What is the connection between the floor and your feet, your ankles, thighs, hips, spine, shoulder blades, neck, back of the arms, hands? Do you have a sense of the shape you are creating as you lie there? If you were on soft sand and you got up, what shape would you see?

3. Concentrate on the internal space between body parts. Can you feel the space between one body part and another? Can you feel the space between your shoulder blades? Between your chin and your chest? Between your ears and your shoulders? Between your shoulders? Between your ribs? Between the vertebrae of your spine? Between your pelvic bones? From your inner thighs to your feet? Between the bones of your feet? Your hands? Can you feel the space between your hands and the sides of your body? Between your legs? Between your feet?

4. Open your eyes and repeat the scan, first with your eyes in soft focus—not necessarily concentrating on any area of the room. Note the experience. Now focus on some point on the ceiling above you. Repeat and note the difference from previous scans.

Stress Release

The more you know about your own tension and where it is located, the more prepared you are to release it. The areas where you carry tension (or increased muscle contraction) have less blood and nerve flow due to their constantly contracted state. This creates an imbalance in your physical function and alignment. Relationships between muscle, bone and neural systems are deeply ingrained from habits related to your present and past environments. To change habits requires a commitment to change your approach.

> *Deep change is a true expansion of the self, a removal of self-imposed limits— restrictions grounded in irrational fears and childhood defeats. These fears must be contacted and re-experienced. The attitudes must be brought to awareness, then re- examined, and the whole process enlightened with persistent self-discovery. A new base must be built up on physical vitality, realistic attitudes, emotional satisfaction, and the acceptance of life.*
>
> **Ron Kurtz, founder of Hakomi Therapy**

It is easy to go to a massage therapist and leave feeling a temporary release of physical and mental tension. And such sessions can be valuable. However, the maintenance of a released relaxed body requires a consistent daily practice that includes breathing, focusing, stretching, strengthening and grounding exercises (see Appendices A, B and C for guidelines).

So if you are used to a specific way of orienting yourself, how do you know when a muscle is being released and you are moving with less tension? There will probably be both sudden, dramatic releases and slow small reorganizations. Bodily stress associated with a highly emotional experience is more likely to create a greater release of tension, than if it is simply related to a habit picked up from being raised within a certain family or geographical area. Results of a sudden change can be frightening: nausea, disorientation, fear, weeping, exhaustion, flashbacks and hallucinations. But it is possible to reduce tension without these effects.

Muscle soreness can be the result of failure to warm up and cool down before and after strenuous exercise, poor mechanical use of the body, stress on the body related to life style or overuse of specific muscle groups. Typically soreness is the result of an accumulation of toxic waste in the muscle tissue. This waste, known as lactic acid, is caused by oxygen deprivation due to some physiological phenomena or to constant anxiety. The situation perpetuates itself in a vicious cycle. Greater anxiety produces more lactic acid, more tense, sore muscles and more anxiety. People in a state of stress are then more likely to injure themselves than those who are in a state of relaxed readiness.

Stress can be positive as well as negative. Positive stress exists when you feel in control of the situation and believe you can influence what is taking place. It is a challenge rather than a throat. You approach it with a combination of commitment and curiosity. Negative stress occurs in a situation where you feel a demand or a threat, resulting in alienation, frustration or hopelessness. You are a victim of circumstances, unable to influence what is taking place in your life.

The question becomes, "How do you deal with negative stress?" Those who do so effectively have developed a variety of coping mechanisms. Joan Borysenko, director of the Mind/Body Clinic at Harvard Medical School, has identified one of these as *transformational* as in transforming the moment. She emphasizes a positive approach to stress management in which people learn to engage the situation with an attitude of exploration and change. (To study more about this approach, visit www.joanborysenko.com.) Stress can be viewed as an opportunity to learn to live with change. Anyone in a stressful situation can benefit from practicing the following:

EXERCISE 2.3 **REDUCING STRESS**

1. Connect with your breath: Be certain you are breathing through the diaphragm and lengthen the phrasing of each breath.
2. Change imagery: Fully acknowledge your current circumstances. Then shift your thoughts away from problems, thinking not about what you do not want, but what you want. Create a strong, complete, empowering sensory image of what you want to have happen that includes aural, visual, kinesthetic components.
3. Move: Get up, walk and unstress by moving your body. Make a quick assessment: What part of your body needs attention right now? Choose a physical activity to fit that need and shift your focus to that. Activity automatically helps to raise your mood.
4. Replenish nutrients: Have a drink of water. Eat a small snack you know gives you energy. Foods for increased mental alertness are low in fat and include protein, resulting in faster thinking, greater energy, increased attention to detail and quicker response time. Foods for increased calmness are low in fat and protein but high in complex carbohydrates such as almonds, avocados, an apple.

This exercise can be combined with activities that take you away from the stress. Combine a walk outside taking in the view with eating a small snack. Combine taking a moment to look at an inspiring section of a book or your journal with some basic warm-up exercises. Have whatever beverage helps rejuvenate you while you take a moment to reflect and note muscular activity. Go for a short walk, normalizing your breathing with your movement. With practice, you can train yourself to look for solutions beyond problems and to focus on what you can control rather than what you cannot. Learning to live with stress will help prevent injury because you will have learned to work with yourself and not against yourself, been specific about your physical approach and listened to your body's signals.

In general, look for opportunities to combine useful activities for optimum use of your time. Numerous options have been suggested in these first two chapters. Here is an example of an exercise that uses time expediently and satisfactorily:

EXERCISE 2.4 **DOUBLE DIPPING, BREATH AND ABS**

This is an opportunity to double dip, combining the practice of deep diaphragmatic breathing with working on your abs, with mutual benefit in both areas.

1. Take a deep breath through your nose and throat far into your diaphragm, allowing an expansion of your lower torso. Let it totally relax out. Feel full and comfortable.
2. Hold that extension for as long as is comfortable and slightly beyond. A count of 25 would be reasonable, but allow yourself to let go at any point.
3. Exhale powerfully while tightening your abdominal muscles enough to feel empty and slightly tense.
4. Hold this "thinnest you have ever been" position the same as 2, pulling in further for the tightest waist you have ever had. As above, 25 counts or what works for you.
5. When it is necessary to inhale, allow the air to explode into your entire middle and expand fully.

Repeat 5–10 times.

Variations:

•   Start with your head tilted slightly forward and as you inhale tilt it backward, then let it drop into your chest as you exhale.
•   Raise your elbows up on either side as you inhale. Let your hands drop back to your side while exhaling.

Healing Your Knowledge

As much as you know about your body, it is now time to increase that knowledge in a move toward expertise. Your instrument is you. Just as the musician and mechanic need a deep and detailed understanding of their instruments to tune or tune up, you want information that will help you pursue a healthy confident state and acquire awareness to develop and maintain an instrument that is truly well tuned. First off, we will define some basic vocabulary terms that may not often be used in your offstage life but are essential to an actor who not only wishes to move well, but to communicate with others through his body. We will then move on to the basic elements of your instrument (bones, joints, muscles) for comprehensive and flexible body wisdom. Here is some basic movement lingo:

Agility—Being capable of moving quickly and easily, nimbleness, the ability to think and act fluidly, acuity of mind and body.

Alignment—The state in which your head, shoulders, spine, hips, knees and ankles relate and line up with each other, putting less stress on your body's structure.

Balance—A comfortable state of equilibrium in which the distribution of weight allows you to remain upright and steady, a condition in which varying elements come together in correct proportion.

Centering—The point from which your core energy flows out as well as the physical and emotional center of the character you are portraying. The centers are most often divided between head, heart and pelvis.

Flexibility—Similar to agility, though it may refer to your capacity to collaborate as well, plus a specific range of motion which you have or are attempting to master.

Gesture—A movement of the body's head and limbs either separately or together.

Grounding—A healthy relationship to gravity, the capacity to plant your weight firmly and confidently. Also confident knowledge as in being well grounded in the facts.

Lines of energy—Muscular patterns and planes of movement, externally as well as within the nervous system.

Musicality—Sensory awareness of tonality, melody, phrasing and tempo.

Neutrality—The capacity to divest yourself of distractions and tendencies that prevent creating a clean slate when preparing to perform.

Posture—The organization of your entire body either standing or sitting.

Release—A state of allowing or enabling restrictions, with the freedom to be here and now.

Spatial awareness—Accurate perception of proximity and relationships, including yourself, others onstage and the audience.

Stamina—Endurance or fortitude, the capacity to not only achieve but sustain a challenging state with assurance and determination.

Stillness—The containment of all the body's energy sources.

Strength—The power to perform challenging actions without undue strain as well as the emotional ability to withstand pressure and thrive.

Transformation—Process by which you change yourself to suit the character or the changes the character undergoes within the arc of the play.

Balance, alignment and grounding are the integration of your body to the force of gravity, which is the attraction between the earth and all on or above its surface. The center of gravity of an object is that imaginary point about which all parts exactly balance each other. In the human body, it is located in the pelvis in front of the upper part of the sacrum (the large, triangular bone at the base of the spine and at the upper, back part of the pelvic cavity) at 55 percent of the height of the individual. To understand how to develop centered alignment, balance and grounding you need to understand the skeletal and muscle system around this point in the pelvis.

Many think of the skeleton as a rigid framework on which all other body parts hang, like a building, a set of building blocks with the skin as walls. However, the human skeleton is a dynamic group of interactive bones whose function is to determine the proper distance between its various parts, and to make certain that spacing is not compromised. For example, the bone in your upper leg preserves a consistent distance between your hip joint and knee cap. This bone, helped by muscles, tendons, ligaments and other soft tissue, allows you to resist gravity and stand upright while providing mobility in the joint that allows you to walk, run, hop or skip. Each bone structure and joint has a specific placement generated by thousands of years of evolution. The space allows the bones to move, the joints and ligaments help to define the parameters of their movement, and the bones, by defining the placement and the function of the flesh around them, define the nature of the movement itself. Alignment is not a static position held as if you were a soldier at attention. Instead of being a position you find and hold, it is a continual act of discovery as you adjust to each new situation.

As an actor you constantly use your imagination to build on a script to create a character and the character's world. Dancers and athletes also use this ability to imagine changing habitual muscle patterns or developing specific skills. A golfer may visualize the perfect stroke over and over again to mentally train muscle memory. Throughout this text, exercises will ask you to use images to help you develop a balanced, aligned, grounded and centered body. Some will use metaphor such as imagining your pelvis as a wheel and slowly reversing the direction from forward to back in order to adjust and balance pelvic alignment. Others will be used in the creation of the physical life of a character.

Your Body's Structure

Great, versatile actors such as Meryl Streep, Daniel Day Lewis and the legendary Vanessa Redgrave (quoted at the opening of this chapter) are constantly changing the organization of their body's structure in the development of a character's physicality. They can do this because they have committed to a regime that insures that they are strong, flexible and aerobically fit. They also have a deep perceptual awareness of the integration of the body's structure and their relationship to personal physical habits. As this awareness deepens, so will your perception of bones to muscle integration as well as how the pelvis, head and joints evolve alignment, centering and balance.

The material which follows is in three sections: first, an exploration that expands your awareness of a specific body part; second, an investigation of your incorporation of the body part in daily activities; third, the observation of how others integrate this body part in daily actions. The combination takes you from a general observation of self and others started in the first chapter to a more specific and detailed set of awarenesses.

Your Skeleton

Bones come in many shapes and sizes depending on their function. The total bony structure is divided into the axial or central skeleton that includes your head, spine and rib cage and the appendicular skeleton of your pelvis, arms/hands and legs/feet. The names derive from the terms central axis and appendages. These two major regions are often studied separately, since the body's central axis has functions distinct from its limbs and girdles or attachment points.

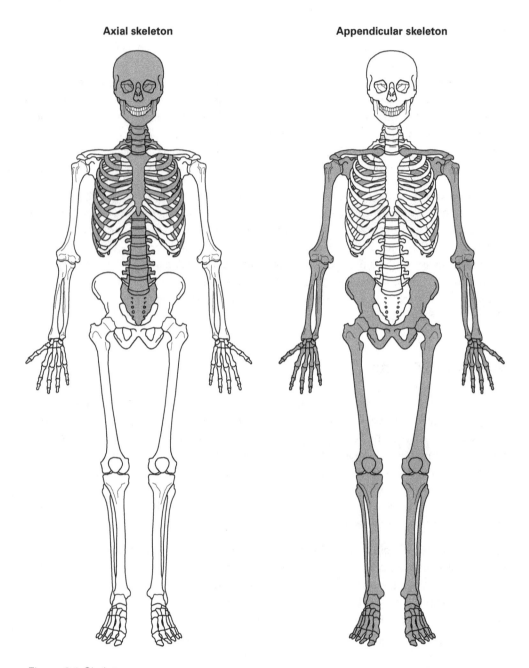

Axial skeleton   **Appendicular skeleton**

Figure 2.1 Skeletons

The axial and appendicular bones form a skeletal framework that protects your vital organs, supports your weight and provides the framework for movement. The bones of the legs are larger and denser than those of the arms, which carry less weight. At the lower end of your spine, in the lumbar region, the bones are denser than those in the upper reaches in the cervical area.

Connecting your bones is an interface of cartilage called a joint. Range of movement between connections varies between body parts and joint function, including immovable joints (such as those of your skull); slightly movable or limited-range joints (as in the spine); and freely movable joints (as in the elbow, wrist, ankle, hip, hand and feet).

EXERCISE 2.5 **DISCOVERING YOUR BONY STRUCTURE**

1. Standing, sitting or lying, gently massage each area of your body from your head to your feet with a focus on feeling and fusing with the bony structures.
2. As you travel through your bony structure, try to get a feeling or kinesthetic sense of its size. What is the exact circumference of the bones of your arms, your rib cage, your pelvis, your legs and your feet?
3. Stand and balance your weight over feet with legs same width as shoulders and toes pointing forward. Complete an internal scan of your bony structure from head to feet.
4. Rock forward and back on your feet. What do you notice in terms of where the weight is placed in your feet? What movement do you note in the rest of the bony structure, in the ankles, the knees, the hips, the pelvis, the spine, the shoulders, the elbows, the wrists?
5. Repeat observation rocking side to side.
6. Repeat observation making a circle of the body that is initiated in the feet.
7. Walk forward and note the sensation of the placement of the feet on the floor. What movement do you note in the rest of the bony structure from feet to head?
8. Purposely walk on the outside of the feet, then the inside of the feet, on your toes, on your heels. What changes do you note in your bone's organization with each style of walking?
9. Come back to standing feet same width apart as shoulders and toes pointing forward. Experience fully the organization of your bony structure.

Your Pelvis

Your pelvis is the structural and emotional center for your alignment. Constructed like a bowl, it is a complex set of bony structures, muscle tissue and nerves that unite your spine and upper body with your feet and legs. Your pelvis is the point around which the entire weight of your body balances. It is impossible for the rest of you to remain in one position if the pelvis is in motion.

Your pelvis consists of the two hip joints and the articulation of the sacrum with the fifth lumbar vertebra of the spine, the sacrum at the back of the pelvis, the ilium forming the sides, the ischium forming the bottom, and the pubis forming the front. There are three points of connection with the rest of your body (the two hip joints and the articulation of the sacrum with the fifth lumbar vertebra of the spine) that allow the pelvis to move as an individual unit.

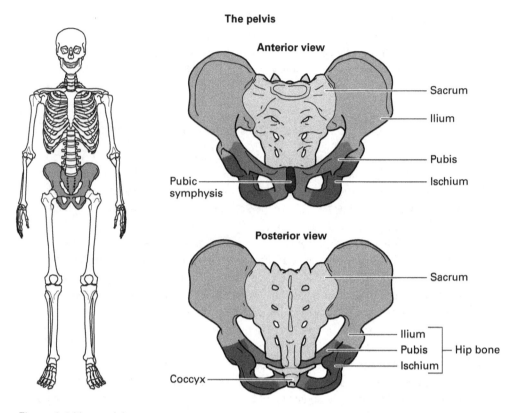

Figure 2.2 Your pelvis

EXERCISE 2.6 **HELLO PELVIS**

1. Lie on your back and slowly draw up your knees toward the ceiling until your feet are parallel to each other, the same width apart as your shoulders and flat on the floor. Begin by slowly tilting your pelvis forward and back in a gentle rocking motion.

2. Now imagine a clock dial painted on the back of your pelvis. Note the figure of six o'clock is drawn on the coccyx and twelve o'clock at the top of the pelvis where it joins the spine at the fifth lumbar vertebra. With these two points in mind, raise the hips so that all of the back of the pelvis is off the floor except the area of twelve o'clock. Now lower the pelvis so that it reverses its direction and the area of twelve o'clock is lifted while the weight of the pelvis rests at six o'clock.

3. Continue to move back and forth between these two points. As you do so, be certain that you are continuing a relaxed breath. Try to answer the following questions: Where is the pressure of my body against the floor as I move my pelvis to twelve o'clock? To six o'clock? What is the role of my feet and legs while completing this movement? Is there a way I could make this movement more economical? More relaxed? More fluid? Is there a way I could incorporate the feet and legs that would make the movement more economical? More relaxed? More fluid?

4. Once you have completed this portion of the exploration, begin to fill the rest of the circular pelvic area with other portions of the clock. You can place three o'clock in the area of the edge of the pelvic bowl on the right, nine o'clock on the left. The other hours will be marked at their appropriate places in between.

5. Begin to explore the entire circle of the clock moving from twelve o'clock, to three o'clock, to six o'clock, to nine o'clock and back to twelve o'clock. Once you have completed this circle, reverse the direction moving first toward nine o'clock. Notice if there are areas of the circle that seem more difficult to move through than others. If you find that it is a fluid circle through the entire perimeter of the clock except from three to six o'clock, return to this area and go back and forth several times trying new methods of incorporating the muscles and the muscles in relationship to the breath until the movement becomes fluid and easy.

6. Follow the initial clock exploration with journeys across the face of the clock from twelve o'clock to five o'clock or three o'clock to nine o'clock.

7. When you have finished exploring the entire pelvic area using the image of the clock, straighten out your legs and complete a scan noticing how you are giving your weight to the floor: it may be the same or different from what it was before the exploration.

8. Return to and repeat a standing body scan noting any changes in awareness of the relationship between the pelvis and the rest of your bony structure.

9. Standing feet same width apart as your shoulders, shift your pelvis side to side, forward and back, a circle that goes from side, to front, to side, to back, to return to side, a circle that goes from side to back to front to side. Can you find the middle of your pelvis with each gesture? What changes do you note in your feet, ankles, knees, hips and spine, as you do each gesture?

10. Walk around the space and observe what happens with your pelvis as you walk going forward, backward, turning. What happens with your pelvis as you sit down?

11. Bring this observation of what happens between pelvis and feet, ankles, knees, hips and spine to your daily activities. What is the integration of the body parts when you are running? Swimming? Sitting in your favorite chair?

12. In your observations of others what do you notice about the integration of the pelvis in standing, walking, sitting?

Your Spine

Your spine is composed of 24 separate vertebrae that can be divided into three groups: the seven cervical vertebrae in the neck area, the twelve thoracic vertebrae in the rib cage area, and the five lumbar vertebrae in the waist and hip area (see Figure 2.3). All three groups share a similar structure but differ in size depending on where they are in the spinal column. In between each vertebra there are disks, which connect, absorb shocks and increase the spine's range of motion. There is also a natural S curve from the head's relationship to the spine and its integration into the pelvis, contributing to the body's balance and alignment.

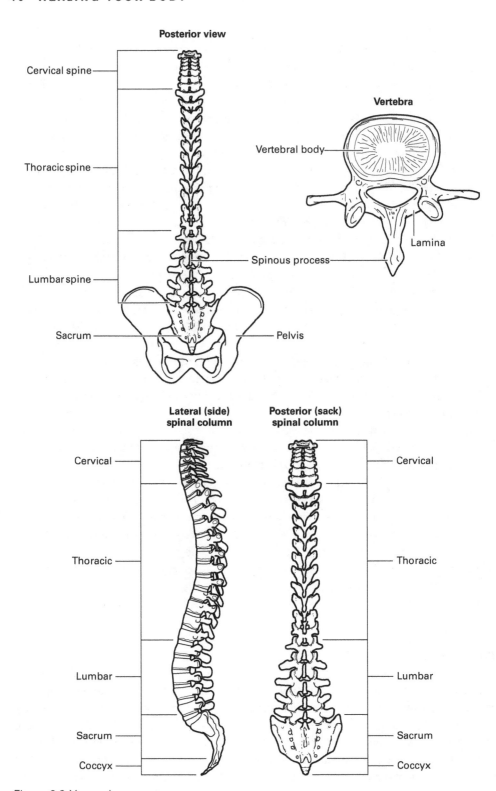

Figure 2.3 Your spine

Organizing a character's physical life often begins with attention to the spine and its relationship to alignment.

The structural functions of your spinal column are to support and transfer weight from the lower to the upper levels of your body and to ensure movement in a variety of directions. Like other flexible columns, it relies on balancing curves that develop after birth. Your spine curves forward in the cervical and lumbar regions and backward in the thoracic and sacral regions. Movements of your spinal column include flexion (forward bending), extension (backward bending), lateral flexion (bending to the side) and rotation.

EXERCISE 2.7 **HELLO SPINE**

Here is a set of suggestions to help you get acquainted with the various regions of your spine and understand how they are functionally integrated. Do not feel limited to the movements given you. Complete each movement becoming aware of the beginning or initiating element of the action and the ending of it. Allow a complete disengagement of the muscles between each movement.

1. Lying on your back, complete a scan.
2. Using the pressure against the floor generated in your heels, begin a gentle rocking motion that moves you up and down from your head to your feet. As you continue moving, observe the vertebrae that have a sense of gentle vibration or rocking in them. Using the knowledge you have of the spinal vertebrae, form a kinesthetic picture of each vertebra from the coccyx through the lumbar region to the thoracic and cervical vertebrae; what does the relationship between the spine and the pelvic bowl feel like?
3. Let the movement slowly drift away.
4. Take your right arm and place it above your head, palm up, and reach it toward the area above your head keeping it on the floor and return it. What vertebrae become engaged as you lift your arm? What is the range of motion? Try it several times.
5. Keeping your arm in the same place, reach your arm upward as you turn your head to the left. What vertebrae did you get acquainted with this time? Did parts of your spine curve as you turned your head? Investigate with the attitude of a child—moving back and forth between arm and head, discovering more about each as you become aware of the integration between the two.
6. Repeat on the other side.
7. With your arms at your sides reach your right arm toward your feet. What vertebrae did you engage this time? Begin a small oval stroking motion on the floor toward your feet and up toward your waist and back. How does this change the engagement with your vertebrae? Repeat. Try it with the other arm.
8. Placing your arm horizontal to the body, move the arm in a slow arc from the waist to above the head. How does this change the relationship? Or, what about lifting the arm above the body and reaching for the arm on the opposite side? Repeat. Try it with the other arm.

9. Lying on your back, bring your knees up. Place your feet flat on the floor. Now drape one leg over the other. Release the legs in the direction of the leg that is on top. Repeat. What vertebrae are part of this action? Try the other leg. Note the sequential engagement of the vertebrae as you twist to one side or the other.

10. Once you have explored the range of these possibilities, lay with your back on the floor and initiate a gentle rocking using the pressure of your heels on the floor; notice how much more of your spine you are aware of. Let go of the rocking gesture and complete a body scan with a focus on your spine.

11. Stand with your feet in parallel and go through a set of actions of bending forward and back, to each side, to each diagonal. Follow this with a twist that is initiated to each side. With each gesture note the integration of the different lumbar, thoracic and cervical vertebrae.

12. Take this observation of your spine to activity in your daily life. What happens when you are sitting in front of the computer? Conversing with friends at a party? Participating in a sports activity?

13. What do you note about other people's integration of their spine during daily activities?

Your Head

Your head contains your primary, sensory channels for survival: your eyes and ears. While hunters and gatherers in past cultures detected the motion of animals through their feet or figured out the weather by the feel of the wind against their skin, you primarily need to be able to interact with machines through touch or voice. The result is head as primary preceptor and as initiator of action. This often creates a contraction in the neck area as you try to complete tasks, such as spending long periods in front of a computer screen, requiring hand–eye coordination.

Although all body therapies consider the head as important in understanding your alignment, the Alexander technique was initially developed to correct a personal problem of the originator, F. Matthias Alexander, regarding the integration of his head with the rest of his body. The basic principles of Alexander are similar to those of good alignment patterns in general. They are as follows:

1. Neck free:

The neck is free when the muscles of your neck and upper back are released while participating in movements of other body parts. Do not try to keep your head in a fixed position. Your head is delicately balanced on top of the spine at the atlanto-occipital joint. This is a pivot joint that allows the head to nod up and down, move side to side, and rotate to the left and right. The head floats on top of the spine as your tail bone at the bottom of the spine releases behind the pelvis and toward the earth. One image of the release of the head is to imagine it as a balloon moving upward and the spine as a string hanging from it.

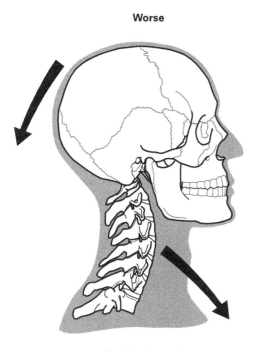

Worse

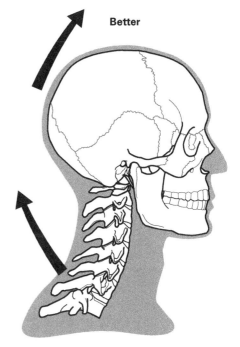

Better

Head being pulled
down and back.

Head releasing
forward and up.

Figure 2.4 Your head

2. Torso long, wide and deep:

    To lengthen your spine does not mean to hold it straight, but to allow the existence of its natural curves. Consider your torso as a hollow tube filled with breath. Your shoulders are allowed to open and widen. Feel the energy of your body flowing outward from the center of your torso all the way through your fingertips. Your hips are released within your joints to move with ease. Your spine lengthens upward as your legs and knees move easily away from your torso. Your legs are not pulled inward toward your pelvis but are grounded into the floor through the soles of your feet.

The goal of the following exploration is to provide a means of experiencing the Alexander principles while lying relaxed on the floor and having someone else guide your body to new modes of understanding by using a gentle massage technique.

EXERCISE 2.8 NECK RELEASE

Working with a partner, do these exercises with one person as the guide, take a brief rest, and then switch. As you are working, sustain an integrated focus that operates on two levels: the focus on the other person and on your own experience.

1. Person A lie on the floor on your back and person B sit in a comfortable position at A's head. Applying a light touch with your hands, change the balance of A's head so that the muscles in the nape of the neck lengthen and the head rotates more comfortably on the shoulders. Do not over-stretch muscles by applying too much pressure. Correctly done, the massage will help to create a new balance in the body.

2. B take a minute to place your hands gently on A's forehead and begin to discover A's breath rhythm and try to integrate it with yours.

3. Next, lift the head, cupping it gently in your hands. Do nothing else at this point until you can feel that A is allowing you to hold the complete weight of her head. Then gently roll the head side to side while easily pulling directly upward along the axis of the spine: do not pull the head so the chin lifts. You will probably notice a release in the muscles of the neck and shoulders.

4. Now stroke and massage the neck. Carefully placing one hand palm down below the base of the neck, massage and pull gradually outward toward the side. You will see the shoulder visibly widen and flatten. Repeat on the other side. Repeat several times in a stroking manner similar to milking a cow or stroking a cat. Gently replace the head on the mat.

5. Going to one side of the body, lift an arm so that it is well supported. Follow this by a gentle jiggle of the arm from the hand into the shoulder socket until A gives up control of the arm to you. Then begin to massage the whole arm, beginning in the center of the back between the scapula, drawing the arm steadily downward and away from the torso, continuing through the hand and into the fingers. Repeat with the other arm.

6. Moving to the leg, lift it, supporting it underneath the thigh area. Repeat the gentle jiggling motion used with the arm, waiting for the person to give you the weight of her leg. Once A has released the leg, begin to pull gently downward as you make little circles of the leg in the hip joint. Do not force anything. If it feels like there is a place where there is a constriction, allow it to be there and work within the range of movement that is of ease for the person. Slowly lower the leg and gently brush from the hip down the outer side of the leg to the feet. Repeat with the other leg.

7. Return to the head to be certain that it has remained free of tension. Placing your hands on either side of A's shoulders do a little jiggle back and forth and then stop to see if it reverberates through the rest of the torso area.

8. Have A roll to either side and come to a sitting position with the torso released to the front, knees relaxed, head dropped. Then slowly bring A to a vertical sitting position using your fingers to walk up the spine from the tail bone up through the last vertebrae in the cervical spine that connects the spine to the head.

9. Help A to stand and, walking behind her, remind her to allow the back of the neck to release upward. Locate the top of the spine at the center base of the head, by placing a finger of each hand in a horizontal position under the opening of the ear and pointing inward. If the fingers were extended toward the center from each side they would meet at the center base of the head at the top of the spine.

10. Switch places and repeat the process.

(Note: For more information on studying the Alexander technique see Chapter 3.)

Your Appendages

Your appendages are attached to the axial skeleton and to each other through a series of joints, each with a particular function. These include the ball and socket joints of the shoulder and hip, the hinge joints of the elbow and knee, the saddle joint of the wrist, and the plane joint of the ankle. The unique movement styles of each joint combine together to contribute to your ability to move through any space in movements that take you away from gravity in jumps, sliding to the side horizontally, walking or running forward and back as well as in a diagonal direction. The motions of the joints of your shoulders, elbows and wrists are the primary means you use to communicate. The motions of the joints of your hips, knees and ankles become pivotal in any situation that requires a decision you make to fight or flight.

Your entire alignment is also influenced by the use of the supporting elements from your pelvic bowl through your hip joints, limbs, knees, ankles and feet. When your lower extremities are in an ideal position, your weight is centered through your pelvis at your hip joints, and your thigh, calf and foot are centered in a forward or neutral position that could be bisected by a line drawn through the centers of the hip, knee and ankle joint.

Slightly bend your knees and observe whether the movement of your knee, ankle and foot fall into the neutral, pronation or supination position by observing the angle of the knee and where the weight is placed on the foot. Repeat the slight bend at the knee several times with a focus on placing the knee in a line from the hip to knee to center of the ankle and foot. Slowly walk around the room and with each step concentrate on the line of relationship between the hip, knee and ankle/foot. This adjustment is most effective when it becomes part of your daily life and one way to adjust this relationship is through the joints.

We tend to view the joints of the body as separate units that are not necessarily integrated with each other. But watch someone with efficient movement patterns completing any physical action and you will observe a complex process as each segment responds to every other segment. Without this level of functional integration, unnecessary restriction of motion occurs. Good joint action exists when there is an equal distribution of force at each joint as the action is carried throughout the body, as when a gesture of the arm includes a clear distribution of energy from the hand through the arm, elbow and shoulder to the front through the center of the body in the vertebrae and through the legs and feet.

EXERCISE 2.9 **BODY JAZZ: JOINT INVESTIGATION**

1. Using your knowledge of your joints and movement, put on your favorite music.
2. Start with the ankles and explore all the potential movements of the ankle by itself and in relationship to the floor. Note how it moves in relationship to the tibia and fibula bones of the leg and articulates with the bones of the foot. Also note the complete range of motion of the ankle forward and back, to the side in a circle. As you investigate the joint, note the very center of its articulation.
3. Follow this up to the saddle joint of the wrist, hinge joints of the knees and elbows, the ball and socket joints of the hips and shoulders. In your exploration, note the

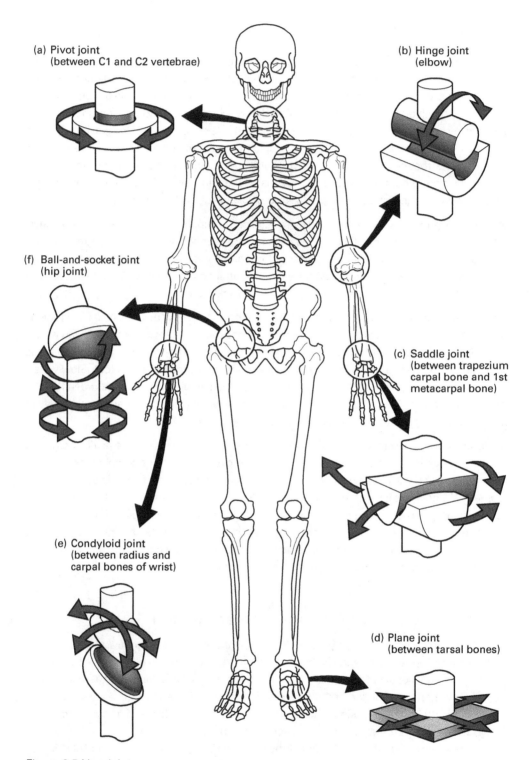

(a) Pivot joint
    (between C1 and C2 vertebrae)

(b) Hinge joint
    (elbow)

(f) Ball-and-socket joint
    (hip joint)

(c) Saddle joint
    (between trapezium
    carpal bone and 1st
    metacarpal bone)

(e) Condyloid joint
    (between radius and
    carpal bones of wrist)

(d) Plane joint
    (between tarsal bones)

Figure 2.5 Your joints

Neutral subtalar
position with neutral
knee alignment

Pronation with
internal rotation
of the knee

Supination with
external rotation
of the knee

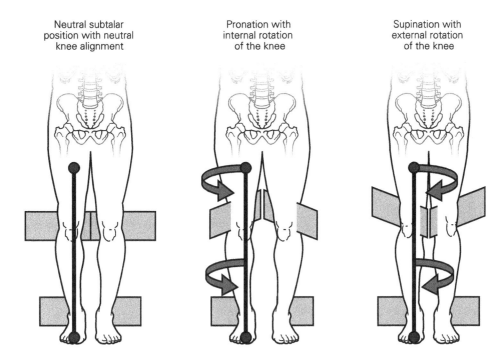

Figure 2.6 Your hips, knees, ankles and feet

range of motion of each joint, the potential implication of movement in other parts of the body's structure related to the joint as well as the center of its articulation.

4. Create a series of sequential gestures that begin in your head and move through your bony structure and each joint. Begin a gesture with your hand and create a series of sequential gestures that move through your bony structure and each joint. Begin a gesture in your knees and expand that gesture to your hips, spine and head.

5. Using your favorite music, continue to explore the gestures of each joint and their relationship to the sequential gestures.

6. Stand feet in parallel position. Note the center point of articulation of your ankles, knees, hips, spinal vertebrae, atlanto-occipital joint where the head attaches, shoulders, elbows and wrists. Walk around the space maintaining awareness of the center of each joint. Stop in a pose and note the center of each joint.

7. Walk very slowly around the space and using the image of the balloon allow the head to release upward and the spine downward and track a line of movement through the joints of your hips, knees, ankles and finally the center line of your foot. Feel the support in the pelvis for the release upward of the head and the alignment of the hip, knee, ankle and foot.

8. Bring the new level of awareness of your joints and their impact on your body's organization to your daily activities. What movements of your joints are involved in sitting? In doing a daily task such as making coffee? Going grocery shopping? Brushing a pet animal?

9. What do you note about the way others use their joints as they complete daily tasks?

Your Muscles

Muscles work in groups to allow, produce and control speed and force, as well as to guide the direction of movement. They also stabilize your central structures against outward pulling force and maintain your body equilibrium as movement changes your distribution of weight. Your muscles in their contracted state produce, retard or prevent movement of your bony system. The two primary muscle groups are the flexors on the interior of the bony structure and the extensors on its exterior or back. They work with your bony structure to allow you to bend and flex your arms, legs and torso, to move your arms and legs in circles as well as forward and back.

Unnecessary or constricted effort, at the time of actual muscle contraction, shortens your body because the overly contracted muscles have a shorter range of motion. This unnecessary contracted state can be the result of an uneconomical use of a body part (usually the consequence of modeling others' movement patterns and incorporating them into your behavior as you grew up), of attempting to protect an injury, or of an imbalance in your system resulting from using some muscle groups more than others. This is often the case with people whose occupations require them to be in one physical position for long periods of time. Common alignment problems are based on an unbalanced use of the muscles and include sway back, lumbar lordosis, thoracic kyphosis or rounded shoulders, forward sagging head. Figure 2.7 includes each of these as well as an example of a balanced alignment. Alignment is achieved by a combination of awareness and new muscle integrations, increasing contraction in some muscles and releasing it in others.

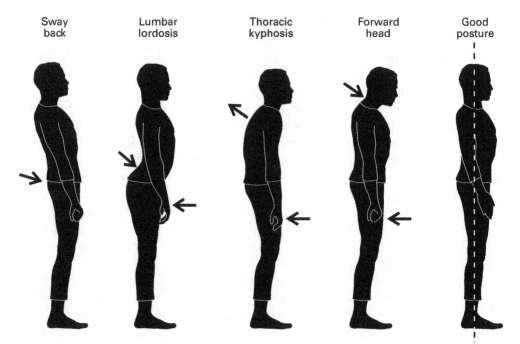

| Sway back | Lumbar lordosis | Thoracic kyphosis | Forward head | Good posture |

Figure 2.7 Muscles and alignment

EXERCISE 2.10 **MUSCLE AWARENESS**

Here is an exploration to help you become more aware of the use of the muscles.

1. Begin by lying down on your back and complete a scan noting how your head and spine are resting on the floor.
2. Gently move first your head from side to side, now lift and lower it. What muscles do you use for each action?
3. Lift your arms up and across your body and return them to the floor. What muscles do you need to use to lift the arms? To put the arms on the floor?
4. Lift first one leg and then the other. What muscles do you need to lift the leg? To put the leg on the floor? Lift both legs and ask the same question.
5. Stand and scan your muscles. In what areas of the body are you using the muscles to maintain an upright stance? Abdomen? Torso? Legs?
6. Begin walking; what muscles are you using to move forward? Backward?
7. Sit in a chair; what muscles are you using to sit down? To get up from the chair?
8. Experiment with standing, walking and sitting with a focus on the muscles in different areas of your body. Try all three actions using just the muscles on the back of the torso, hips, legs. The front of the torso, hips, legs.
9. Have someone take a photo of yourself in profile standing, walking, sitting. Using Figure 2.7 as a guide, which category would you place yourself in?
10. Observing those around you and using Figure 2.7 as a guide, what category would you place them in?

Online

Depending on the answer to question 9 above, you will want to incorporate into your daily practice a focus on adjusting the muscular use of your body. Learning to release the contraction of muscle groups can be achieved by increased awareness, incorporating muscle strength and stretch work into your workout and including images encouraging new muscle organization.

The position of your pelvis and the muscles of your spine are related. Unbalanced posture is often the result of tightness in the muscles of the lower back or failure to widen and lengthen the muscles of the back, with a corresponding narrowness in the muscles of the region of the shoulder blades. The following images will help you release tension in the lower back while increasing tonus in the abdominal muscles. The more detail you add to the image in terms of size, color and other imagery, the more you will succeed in re-patterning your muscles.

EXERCISE 2.11 **MUSCLE RE-PATTERNING**

To lengthen the spine downward:

1. Feel your back resting on a warm flat surface with your buttocks sliding away from you as the warmth spreads from the center of your back toward your tail bone.

2. Feel the bony structure on each side of the pelvis as a rotating disk that is slowly moving back and down as it takes the energy from behind the belly button and sends it out the tail bone.

To widen the back and release the upper torso:

1. Experience the rib cage as a toy accordion with handles on each side just under the arms and vertical pleats on the front and back.
2. Feel the gentle pressure of the accordion closing inward toward the center until it is no wider than your neck.
3. Pay particular attention to the opening of the pleats in the back, especially the center of the back.

Dynamic Neutral

There are three masks:
The one we think we are,
the one we really are,
and the one we have in common.

Jacques Lecoq, physical acting pioneer

Dynamic neutral is an idea that originated with the training theories of legendary French innovator Jacques Lecoq through his École Internationale de Théâtre. This notion of neutral includes:

- Your are a blank page, holding no cultural ideas concerning correct behavior for a given situation.
- You are the I/Not I.
- You are neither masculine nor feminine.
- You belong to no social group, nor hold a particular religious view of the world.
- You have not developed a specific sense of the past or the future but only the ongoing present.
- You incorporate psychological, emotional and physical aspects that include detachment, non-judgment, alignment, physical and emotional balance, openness, acceptance, internal and external focus, and the ability to listen and breathe through your entire self.

Neutral is a conceptual image not a precise state. In learning to embody neutral as an image, you become rooted in the core of your essential being. You allow yourself to be an empty vessel, a container for possibilities and dynamic potential, a conduit for character. This potential comes from the core of your own uniqueness as you stand on the edge of the "cliff of possibilities" of your imagination. The following exercises are devised to help you achieve a dynamic aligned neutral. Neutral is a state you begin each exercise in the following chapters and return to at the end of each exercise.

(More information on Lecoq is provided in Chapter 3.)

EXERCISE 2.12 CONSTRUCTIVE REST

1. This is an alignment exercise evolved from the work of Lulu Sweigard (1895–1974) titled Ideokinesis. Take a position on your back with your knees bent and pointed at the ceiling. Allow your knees to be slightly further apart than your hips but with your feet still on the floor.

2. Allow your knees to drop toward each other so they are resting somewhere in the center line of your body. If your knees tend to fall away from each other, take a piece of rope or material and tie the knees together. The upper part of your torso and head should be resting comfortably on the floor.

3. Take your arms and reach them toward the ceiling, then allow them to fall across the front of the body so that they are crossing each other. (You may find that your chin reaches toward the ceiling in this position. If this is the case, try putting a folded towel under your head to see if it brings your chin toward your chest and your head in better alignment with your spine.)

4. Savor this body position in which the different muscle groups need to use the least amount of contractual effort to maintain an ongoing relationship with each other. It is also a position in which you can be actively engaged in an imagistic task without being likely to go to sleep.

Figure 2.8 Constructive rest

EXERCISE 2.13 **THE EMPTY SUIT**

1. Once you have achieved the constructive rest position, begin to focus on your diaphragmatic breathing. Once a breath phrase has developed, begin to focus on the images associated with the empty suit.
2. The empty suit is made out of a fabric that you would like to have close to your skin. The suit is one piece with bell shaped trousers with tassels at the end of the legs. The coat portion has a soft circular collar with a zipper that extends up the front from the pelvis to the top of the Chinese collar.
3. Imagine yourself as a suit in which the trousers are supported at the knees by the cross of an imagined hanger suspended from the ceiling; the arms of the coat rest across the front of the coat. The suit has many wrinkles in it. To straighten out this wrinkled suit, you must imagine the following images as if they were occurring.

THE TROUSERS

1. Feel the upper part of the thigh of the trousers falling together as your knees are supported over the bar of the hanger. Feel the crease of the suit's fabric at the thigh joint sink into the empty seat of the trousers.
2. Feel the trouser leg twist inward across the front until the long crease is in the mid-front centering with the knee and thigh joint. Concentrate on one trouser leg at a time and feel the length of the crease from the ankle to the thigh.
3. Feel the looseness of the bell-shaped lower trouser leg as it sags together in folds.
4. Experience the foot as a tassel, made up of different lengths of thread or yarn (long toward the toes, shorter at the heel); watch the tassels release on the floor around the edge of the foot.

THE COAT

1. As you start to zip the zipper, feel the crosswise wrinkles on the back of the coat being smoothed downward from the lower part of the back and slowly moving upward. Feel the vertical wrinkles on the back of the coat at the inner borders of the shoulder blades being smoothed outward until the coat becomes very broad shouldered. Finally, feel how good it feels to have the fabric of the coat smoothed down the back and beyond the tail bone.
2. Now feel the zipper in the front of the coat being closed to the top of the soft Chinese collar.

THE SOFT COLLAR

Feel the crosswise wrinkles in the collar being smoothed upward until the top of the collar reaches the base of the head.

THE EMPTY HEAD

Feel your head as a large, empty ball filled with breath. Can you feel the distance between your ears, and from front to back at the level of your head? What follows is a checklist of points to remember in terms of creating a centered, grounded alignment.

EXERCISE 2.14 **LET GO, LIE DOWN**

1. This is about releasing and opening, letting go of your everyday concerns.
2. Let go by one or more of the following: focus on the breath, various forms of shaking out the joints, both lying and standing, and yoga poses or other stretches that open up the body.
3. Release the joints—neck release, rolls and manipulations of the joints as individual units and together, or jiggling of the joints.

EXERCISE 2.15 **LINK UP**

Linking up or grounding is finding the dynamic connection of your alignment through nine lines of movement embedded in the empty suit exercise.

1. Lengthen your spine downward.
2. Shorten the distance between your mid front pelvis and rib cage.
3. Shorten the distance from the top of your sternum to the top of your spine.
4. Narrow your rib cage.
5. Widen the back of your pelvis.
6. Narrow the front of your pelvis.
7. Feel connection from the center of your knee to the center of your hip joint.
8. Feel connection from the big toe to heel.
9. Lengthen the central axis of your trunk upward.

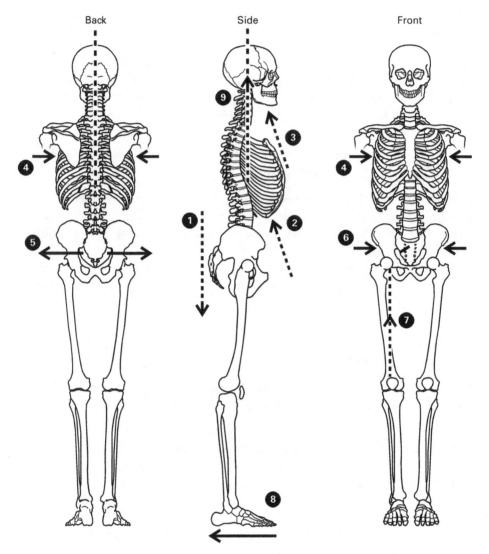

Figure 2.9 The nine lines of movement

Summary

Before reading this chapter, you probably had a tentative acquaintance with your body's structure. We hope that relationship has now become deeper and richer, with a significantly expanded awareness. We hope you are beginning to develop a program for fitness and health that will allow your body to respond to a large range of movement challenges. We know you can use the basic vocabulary terms for insight and interaction, whenever you need to identify what is going on physically. Your awareness of the relationship between your skeletons, the integrating role of the pelvis, the dynamic organization of the spine, the release of the head, and the unique function of each joint should inform new steps. All these you can bring to the warm-up you learned in Chapter 1 or any other. You should, at the end of a warm-up, be able to register your body's general alignment from the standpoint of neutral, a point of return as you move into and out of characters.

Options regarding your anatomy can become part of your daily interactions at home and in the world, including ways to prevent injury from misuse. These options will give you greater control, increase your potential power as a performer and grant you the capacity to make mindful choices. The increased awareness is also valuable in expanding your observational skills of people in general. And actors thrive on control, power and choice. You are on your way to using your entire physical self to become a better actor!

CHAPTER 3 MOVEMENT MASTERS

Movement Masters

Examining the leading innovators and disciplines in actor movement training

Exploring all these ways to awaken your body's potential can be thrilling and confusing at first, but then you find unexpected connections and far greater choice opening up to you.

Meryl Streep, actor

Somatics

We believe and hope you will agree that movement training should be somatic. This term was coined by movement therapist Thomas Hanna in the 1980s from the Greek as "living organism in its wholeness." Hanna aimed to integrate mind and body, the opposite of current Cartesian mind–body dualism. While it took some time to find an appropriate name, somatic inclusion in performance training can be traced to the turn of the twentieth century when Constantin Stanislavski incorporated yoga training into his acting studio and then expanded into other mind/body/emotion connections. Other prominent somatic advocates were movement practitioners Frederick Matthias Alexander and Moshe Feldenkrais, philosopher John Dewey, educator Rudolf Steiner, dancer Isadora Duncan, who challenged the culturally limited vocabulary of the ballet, and dance educators Mabel Todd and Lulu Sweigard who developed new methods of dance training focusing on kinesthetic awareness and visualization.

A somatic approach to performance training now includes a variety of Asian physical disciplines and other physical disciplines that are offshoots of these, such as Pilates, Rolfing, Neuro Linguistic Programming, hybrid forms, massage, meditation, visualization and contemplative practice. All somatic methods promote the self as inseparable from the body and involve learning to listen and live inside your sensations and related deep internal connections. The ultimate goal is being in the present moment and the opportunity this provides to note previous habits and transform them in the building of new skills and competencies.

We offer you here numerous paths to find your own somatic growth program. There are almost limitless ways to work on your body, but some innovators have had a major impact on your training and deserve your attention. As a student of movement you will want to feel conversant with the ideas of those who have been most influential in shaping this discipline and also the various options actors choose to supplement basic training. What follows are the big names in actor movement, our greatest discoverers and teachers, followed by those other important movement areas less identified with an inventor.

Innovators

These artist/educators were able to find new ways to enliven and enrich theatre. Their influence is vast and varied. Each woke us up to other, more exciting possibilities.

1. Frederick Matthias Alexander (1869–1955)

Significance

Alexander was a Shakespearean actor who developed a problem with his vocal delivery. After doctors found no physical cause, he began to observe his behavior with a set of mirrors while he was speaking to see if he could discover the problem. He determined that a habitual pattern of head and neck integration disrupted his body's posture and his breath. Over time, he found that an adjustment of the head, neck and spine and general release in the upper torso resolved the problem. He refined his technique and started a practice that he outlined in a series of books.

Key Ideas

The Alexander technique is distinct in that it is the only somatic approach that evolved from the physical life of a performer. Thus, it has embedded in its process a framework that is close to the experience of the actor. Including the following:

1.   Constructive Conscious Control or the need for external observers to act as a mirror for the participant.
2.   End-gaining is to focus on the actual experience and not the goal.
3.   Inhibition or the conscious awareness to move beyond habitual ways of moving in order to free the capacity for the new.
4.   Primary control is a focus on the primary unit of the head, neck and spine with an expansion to the rest of the body.
5.   Psychophysical unity is the unification of thinking and attention in the creation of an action.

Contribution

The Alexander technique is taught by vocal coaches and musicians as it allows for the free alignment of all aspects of the vocal tract by consciously increasing air flow. The technique is also used extensively by actors for its release of the vocal tract as well as the associated relaxation that reduces stage fright.

To Read More

F. Matthias Alexander and Edward Maisel, *The Alexander Technique: The Essential Writings of F. Matthias Alexander* (New York: Carol) 1990.

Michael J. Gelb, *Body Learning and Introduction to the Alexander Technique* (New York: Henry Holt) 1996.

Bill Connington, *Physical Expression on Stage and Screen: Using the Alexander Technique to Create Unforgettable Performances* (London: Bloomsbury Methuen) 2014.

2. Anne Bogart (1951–)

"A great actor seems dangerous, unpredictable, full of life and differentiation," says Anne Bogart, whose most defining work is a series of exercises called "Viewpoints."

Significance

Working to create flexible actor/athletes, Bogart has conceived a whole vocabulary of body use that trains actors to respond to a wide range of challenges and provides them with tools for performing distinctly nonrepresentational works. The nine Viewpoints are points of awareness each performer has while working.

Figure 3.1 Anne Bogart. As much as anyone working today, Bogart has greatly expanded the possibilities of the actor's body in time and space. Copyright photographer Ellen M. Rosenbery.

Four of them relate to *time*:

1. *Tempo:* The speed of movement.
2. *Duration:* How long a movement, gesture or sequence actually lasts.
3. *Kinesthetic response:* The timing of your responses to stimuli.
4. *Repetition:* Repeating something onstage, both internally (within your own body) and externally (something picked up outside your body).

The final five Viewpoints are those of *space*:

5. *Shape:* Lines, curves and mixtures of these two, stationary versus moving shapes, taking on one of three forms: the body in space, the body in relationship to architecture and the body forming a shape with other bodies.
6. *Gesture:* Work involving two different kinds: behavioral (everyday real ones) and expressive (abstract, large ones).
7. *Architecture:* The physical environment where the acting occurs. It includes solid mass (walls, floors, ceilings, furniture, windows, doors), texture (wood, metal, fabric, changing or unchanging textures), light (sources and shadows), color. Within architecture, spatial metaphors (such as "I'm up against the wall" or "lost in space") are created.
8. *Spatial relationship:* Distances between all things onstage, implications of clustering, spreading, focusing.
9. *Floor pattern* (sometimes referred to as "topography"): How the landscape is created by movement, with various areas perhaps assigned greater or lesser density or simply being declared off-limits.

> *In a culture where the best acting is done from the neck up, Anne's work is an obvious antidote . . . It's dance done by actors in the service of dramaturgy.*
>
> **Jon Jory**

Key Ideas

Viewpoints' goals are "listening" with the entire body, achieving spontaneity, taking in and using everything around you, finding larger possibilities, eliminating any "My character would never do that" tendencies, giving up overly cerebral work, and giving yourself surprise, contradiction and unpredictability.

Viewpoints training is about using whatever space you are working in as a source, responding fully to all the elements within it, being vividly aware of movement, refining your capacity for working closely with others and enhancing your sense of how space is altered by choice.

In training or rehearsal, actors may work on a single Viewpoint for an extended period and then begin to layer them. They may be used as purely abstract exercises or centered around ideas in a script. They may be used as warm-ups or ensemble exercises, but also to create the basic staging for a play script. In any script, Viewpoints might be employed to define the use of space and to specifically stage dream sequences, fantasies and other flights of imagination within the whole, whenever nonfacsimile performance is appropriate.

Contribution

Bogart's work is extremely movement-centered, with the spoken word less a key player. She fills up the stage like a moving painting; words sometimes become superfluous. She encourages actors to create a physical score that exists independently from the verbal expression of their characters. In fact, she actively seeks tension between action and word rather than coherence. Her work has been strongly influenced by Asian theatre forms and martial arts. Her teaching methods draw heavily from t'ai chi—nonautocratic, noninterference, being open to what every other has to offer, letting go of restrictive investments of self. Through her "technique of dissociation," she discards Western representational conventions and is regarded by many as our most postmodern innovator. Yet, she also identifies American vaudeville and dancer Martha Graham as primary influences. Regarding her distant inspirations, she says, "I get closest to my American roots by going away."

To Read More

Anne Bogart, *And Then You Act* (New York: Routledge) 2007.
Anne Bogart and Tina Landau, *The Viewpoints Book* (New York: Theatre Communications Group) 2005.
Anne Bogart, *The Director Prepares* (New York: Routledge) 2002.
Michael Bigelow Dixon and Joel A. Smith (eds.), *Anne Bogart View-points* (Lyme, NH: Smith and Kraus) 1995.

3. Michael Chekhov (1891–1955)

One of three "artistic sons" of Constantin Stanislavksi (along with Meyerhold and Vakhtangov), the nephew of the legendary playwright Anton Chekhov was widely admired for being able to become wildly eccentric in performance without ever losing believability. He managed to develop ways for other actors to accomplish the same, using Don Quixote as a model for employing brilliant and even feverish imagination to transform the commonplace into the magical. He left Russia in 1927 and worked in numerous countries. His professional career as an actor brought him to Hollywood, where he was nominated for an Oscar for his role in Hitchcock's *Spellbound*.

Significance

Chekhov placed more emphasis on imagination than Stanislavski had. He encouraged actors to move past emotional memories from their own lives to imaginary events and images, to seek stimulus from totally fanciful experiences, impossible in a literal world but highly suggestive. For example, actors might be led to achieve a sense of giddiness and joy by imagining that they were walking on clouds or a rainbow with almost none of the gravitational limitations they would feel on Earth.

Key Ideas

- *Atmospheres:* A source of moods and waves of emotion from one's surroundings, a relationship or an artwork, equivalent to musical keys.
- *The Higher Ego:* Creative individuality that makes each actor's performance of a role different from that of any other actor, including a sense of ethics, sensitivity, control, compassion and humor, which free them from the restrictions of the narrow, selfish ego.
- *The Psychological Gesture (PG):* A physical action that reveals the inner feelings and personality of the character. For example, a character with great ambition but constant self-doubt might rise from a chair and then immediately sit down again. Although the actor might do this several times throughout the performance as a kind of defining physical manifestation of a troubling psychological state, it will far more likely remain a rehearsal device. This PG might also become a single move, with half the actor's body reaching up and out while the other half clings to the chair and safety. At various moments, the audience might sense an impulse of this kind without the actor actually standing up and sitting down, so that the PG provides a subterranean support for basic character urges.

Contribution

His Psychological Gesture, used throughout the world, is Chekhov's shining achievement, though he also influenced our use of abstract, fanciful, even illogical imagery to achieve effects. What we now call *conditioning forces* originated with Chekhov, though he never named it. All our behavior is based on two immediate influences: physical (such as a sweltering hot day or a brisk one) and psychological (a feeling of foreboding or a sense of playfulness). Both change how we might do the simplest act, such as combing our hair or buttoning a shirt.

He influenced acting teachers to unleash imaginative and fantastical elements, promoting the idea of each performance during the run of a show being different and to some degree improvisational. His use of visualization has become nearly universal.

To Read More

Michael Chekhov, *To the Actor* (New York: Routledge) 2002.
Michael Chekhov, *The Path of the Actor* (New York: Routledge) 2005.
Michael Chekhov, *On the Technique of Acting* (New York: Harper Collins) 1991.

4. Moshe Feldenkrais (1904–1984)

The Feldenkrais method was developed in response to a recurring knee issue derived from playing soccer. It is a movement pedagogy in which the individual is taught to increase their kinesthetic and proprioceptive self-awareness of the function of movements. In this regard, the Feldenkrais method is a constant state of exploration and discovery. The end result is greater ease of movement.

Significance

Feldenkrais is used to improve movement patterns rather than to treat specific injuries or illnesses. This holistic focus means that the primary intention is not to treat injuries. However, it can be used as a type of integrative medicine because correcting habitual movement patterns can help heal an injury. The Feldenkrais practitioner teaches new patterns of movement using a set of slow repetitions that increasingly expand the engagement of body parts.

Key Ideas

There are three key ingredients to a Feldenkrais experience: slowness that allows for increased attention to and awareness of movement, repetition that encourages a deepening of awareness, and explorations that begin with one area of the body and expand to include others.

Contribution

Along with the Alexander technique, the Feldenkrais method is the somatic approach most often incorporated into acting programs. For the actor, it provides a unique method of somatic exploration that can be incorporated into other areas of movement training from learning movement systems such as Laban or skills such as combat and circus.

To Read More

Moshe Feldenkrais, *Awareness through Movement* (New York: Harper) 2009.
Moshe Feldenkrais, *The Potent Self* (New York: Frog Books) 2002.

5. Jerzy Grotowski (1933–1999)

Grotowski was a hugely innovative Polish theatre director and theorist whose approaches to actor training and theatrical production had a profound influence on theatre today.

Significance

He was a major pioneer in the evolution of experimental theatre and the conceptual director, for whom the script is simply a vehicle to explore and achieve something far different than that intended by the playwright. Scripts were radically cut, rearranged, interspersed with bits of other text, and made subservient to the director's intent, often deconstructed or problematized to place the emphasis on a formerly minor area of concern. Sometimes the script would not exist but was evolved through games, experimentation and group effort. Grotowski woke us up to other possibilities.

His work with his Laboratory Theatre in Poland, beginning in 1959, influenced the freedom with which subsequent directors have altered the text. His ideas are considered a direct inspiration for what is now known as Performance Art.

Key Ideas

Grotowski trained his actors to be *überathletes*: physically and emotionally tuned to survive great demands of stamina; open to finding the shock, terror and danger in any moment of a play; and always moving beyond mundane everyday behavior into the extraordinary. He demanded a grueling dedication that made his actors resemble some combination of warriors and priests.

He would also rearrange the relationships of actor and audience so that the latter might be looking down into a pit at the action onstage, or be surrounded by the actors, or countless other nontraditional configurations, which have subsequently been employed by many others.

Contribution

Grotowski reclaimed the vitality of live theatre at a time when media threatened its very identity. His seminal book *Towards a Poor Theatre* (1968) declared that theatre should not, because it could not, compete against the overwhelming spectacle of film and should instead focus on the very root of the act of theatre: actors co-creating the event of theatre with its spectators.

> *Theatre – through the actor's art in which the living organism strives for higher motives – provides an opportunity for what could be called integration, the discarding of masks, the revealing of the real substance: a totality of physical and mental reactions. This opportunity must be treated in a disciplined manner, with a full awareness of the responsibilities it involves. The actor can only accomplish this through an encounter with the spectator – intimately, visibly, in direct confrontation with him, and somehow "instead of" him. The actor's opening up, is an invitation to the spectator, an act of the most deeply rooted, genuine love between two human beings. It epitomizes the actor's deepest calling.*

To Read More

Jennifer Kumiega, *The Theatre of Grotowski* (London: Methuen) 1987.
Thomas Richards, *At Work with Grotowski on Physical Actions* (London: Routledge) 1995.
Lisa Wolford and Richard Schechner, *The Grotowski Sourcebook* (London: Routledge) 1997.

6. Rudolf von Laban (1879–1958)

The Laban method of movement analysis and training was developed by dance artist and theorist Rudolf von Laban. Beyond being one of the pioneers of modern dance in early twentieth century Europe, he evolved a system of movement analysis referred to as Labanotation and a related form of movement study, LMA or Laban Movement Analysis.

Significance

The ideas of Laban are important from the standpoint of notation and application. The Laban method of notation was the first system that allowed for detailed notation of a dance that was comparable to music notation. Laban Movement Analysis was the first system that combined an approach that included total body connectivity with an orientation to weight, space, time and flow.

Key Ideas

Laban Movement Analysis is generally divided into these categories:

1. The total connectivity/integration of the body in which a movement in one area influences movement in other areas as it is realized in mobility/stability, inner/outer, function/expression and exertion/recuperation.
2. Effort/Shape dynamics associated with the weight (strong to light), space (direct to indirect), time (sudden to sustained) and flow (bound to free).

Contribution

It is our opinion that, with the possible exception of Stanislavski, no one has offered more illuminating and useful ideas for movement training than Laban. His effort/shape system has been incorporated into acting programs around the globe as an integrated system of movement training and analysis. The variety of qualities it encourages in the psychophysical life of actors provides a basis for the development of physically articulate characters. Laban's ideas will be further detailed in both chapters 4 and 7.

To Read More

Rudolf von Laban and Lisa Ullmann, *Mastery of Movement* (Rome: Pre Textos) 2011.
Jean Newlove, *Laban for Actors and Dancers* (London: Nick Hern Books) 2007.
Barbara Adrian, *Actor Training the Laban Way* (New York: Allworth Press) 2008.

7. Jacques Lecoq (1921–1999)

Lecoq began gymnastics at seventeen and through work on the parallel bars and the horizontal bar he came to see and to understand the movement of the body through time and space. Later he joined the Comédiens de Grenoble and the Commedia dell'arte. It was in his work in Italy with Commedia that he learned to work with masks.

Significance

In 1956, he opened L'École Internationale de Théâtre Jacques Lecoq in Paris. His program brought people from across the globe to study his style of mask work and also to study architecture, scenography and stage design at his Laboratoire d'Étude du Mouvement.

Lecoq aimed at training his actors in ways that encouraged them to investigate modes of performance that expanded their personal creativity. His training began with the neutral mask with the goal of increasing the actor's awareness of physical mannerisms. Once the actors had mastered the neutral mask, they would be given a series of character masks, each designed to help them expand their ability to physically embody a character.

Key Ideas

Three of the principal skills that he encouraged in his students were *le jeu* (playfulness), *complicité* (togetherness) and *disponibilité* (openness). These skills could only be achieved once the actor embodied a state of neutral and its implied state of no expectations and no judgment.

Contribution

Jacques Lecoq's value to the actor is twofold. First, the concept of neutral is a means to limit habitual behaviors; second, the sequence of character masks which the actor was expected to embrace with an attitude of playfulness and openness but with the realization you were always working with others.

To Read More

Jacques Lecoq and Jean-Gabriel Carasso, *The Moving Body: Teaching Creative Theatre* (New York: Routledge) 2002.
Jacques Lecoq, *Theatre of Movement and Gesture* (New York: Routledge) 2006.
Simon Murray, *Jacques Lecoq* (New York: Routledge) 2003.

8. Vsevolod Meyerhold (1874–1940)

Meyerhold's ideas were too extreme for many in the Russian theatrical community (Stanislavski sometimes referred to him as his "prodigal son") and for various government regimes. He repeatedly incurred the displeasure of authorities, was arrested, exiled and died (and may have been executed) in 1940.

Significance

Meyerhold sensed a fatal flaw in many of Stanislavski's actors—a lack of physical expressivity. He turned to commedia, pantomime, circus, Kabuki, Noh drama, boxing and gymnastics to help train the actor's body to respond fully. From the Eastern theatre, he took the idea of centers of gravity; from clowning, ideas for the expressive mask, exaggeration, foolishness; from pantomime, an actor's need to develop strength and flexibility; from commedia, the idea of mastering *lazzi*, or bits; and from all of these, committing to theatrical excitement. He felt that art is not an imitation of life, with audience members looking through a keyhole, but, rather, always something more. He always asked what was theatrical about theatre and pursued it. He rejected naturalism as irrelevant. He sought an Expected Unexpectedness in which actors bring a sense of mystery and anticipated excitement to their work.

Key Ideas

- *Constructivism:* The set as playground, its bare bones uncovered, even flaunted, many different performance levels and possible routes, with actors "playing" in highly gymnastic fashion.
- *Biomechanics:* A way of training actors to convey emotion, desire, movement and gesture through rhythm, dynamics, economy and focused attention, employing their bodies as expressions in space. Exercises that produce an actor/athlete/machine/clown (not with the improvisational freedom we often associate with clowning but more a mastery of clown techniques). Mind and body are disciplined to acrobatic precision. Biomechanics trains balance, physical control, rhythmic awareness, in both space and time, responsiveness to one's partner, the audience, the ability to attend closely and to react.
- *Sixteen Études:* A series of precise exercises containing all the basic expressive situations in which an actor might be asked to respond.
- *The Acting Cycle:* Intention, Realization and Reaction, Refusal or Point of Repetition.

Contribution

Meyerhold developed a purely external path to emotion: surface to core—an arousal of feeling from the outside. His concern was not for the inner life of the character/actor but for the response of the observer. His work was a constant reminder that creation of feeling in the audience is far more important than that within the actor. He continued a long tradition that emotions are not necessarily felt but shown in performance, a direct link back through Delsarte (1811–1871) to Quintilian (first century A.D.).

His insistence on bare-bones theatre helped clear out the clutter and unessential elements that tended to burden older theatres. He drew in physical disciplines that constitute the body training part of acting programs today and his concept of actor/athlete is widely embraced. His emphasis on the lower body was adapted by Michael Chekhov and then picked up many years later by Tadashi Suzuki.

To Read More

Edward Braun, *Meyerhold on Theater* (New York: Hill and Wang) 1969.
Robert Leach, "Meyerhold and Biomechanics," *Twentieth Century Actor Training*. Edited by Alison Hodge (Now York: Routlodgo) 2000.

9. Constantin Stanislavski (1863–1938)

Stanislavski is considered the single greatest and most influential of all acting teachers. No one has had greater influence on the way the art is studied.

Significance

He created the only known complete system for putting together a character, and it is used to some degree by every reputable acting program. He was a brilliant actor, director and teacher

Figure 3.2 Constantin Stanislavski's impact has been greater than that of any other acting expert. He invented characterization as we know it and laid the basis for actor training as we practice it.

who co-founded the Moscow Art Theatre (MAT) in 1898 and changed the way actors worked forever. Stanislavski wrote four famous books (*An Actor Prepares*, *Building a Character*, *Creating a Role* and *My Life in Art*), which eventually make their way into the personal library of almost any serious student of acting. There is no relaxation, concentration, imagination exercise, no warm-up, no improv, no script experiment currently practiced for which the basic principle and at least the germ of the exercise itself does not appear in these works.

To serve the plays being done by MAT (by writers like Anton Chekhov and Maxim Gorky) that cried out for truth in acting instead of the more extravagant and bombastic attacks many actors had been using at that time, Stanislavski developed a twenty ingredient system designed to produce honest and compelling performances.

Key Ideas

The first ten ingredients are true of any single encounter between people in life and characters in a play: 1. Relationship, 2. Objective, 3. Obstacle, 4. Strategy, 5. Tactics, 6. Text, 7. Subtext, 8. Interior Monologue, 9. Evaluations and 10. Beats—all of which constitute the actor's fundamental vocabulary. Stanislavski determined that in any situation we always make choices based on our feelings about others around us (relationship). You have something you want (objective), something in the way (obstacle) and an ever-changing (tactics) plan to get what you want (strategy). You experience words spoken (text) but also other meanings implied (subtext), with a series of words going on in your head (interior monologue). You consider saying a number of things (evaluations) that you end up rejecting along the way. Any human encounter can be broken down into sections (beats), when changes (a shift in topic, method of persuasion, someone arriving or leaving, an uncovering of new information) occur. Therefore, instead of being one long, confusing blur, any encounter can be experienced in easily understood parts.

If an actor really does each of these things, his attention will be fully engaged, his instrument will respond honestly and he will be compelling to watch. Tension, stiffness and self-consciousness fall away because the mind can only hold so much and these ingredients fill it.

The intitial ten ingredients define an individual scene or human encounter. The remaining ten ingredients encompass the whole of the character before and during the play or an entire personality. They are: 11. Given Circumstances, 12. Magic If, 13. Super Objective and Objective Hierarchy, 14. Through-Line of Actions, 15. Score, 16. Endowment, 17. Recall, 18. Images, 19. External Adjustments and 20. Creative Mood.

If you wish to inhabit someone else, you:

11. Learn all the relevant facts that influence this person's behavior (*given circumstances*).
12. Use these facts to place yourself inside his life perspective (*magic if*).
13. From his point of view, determine what he wants most in life (*super objective*) and his range of lesser but still important goals, both conscious and unconscious (*objective hierarchy*).
14. Experience his particular way of dealing with a variety of obstacles and setbacks. Find the connection between all the moments when a psychological motive prompts a physical impulse, through rehearsal experimentation, until a pattern emerges (*through-line of actions*).
15. Write down the results in manuscript form, and mark the script into workable units (*score*).
16. Project onto people and objects, real and imagined, qualities from your imagination and experience that bring them to life (*endowment*).
17. Use your five senses to awaken memories of both physical sensations and emotions that can be filtered into the character's feelings (*recall*).
18. Add to your constantly playing interior monologue a film of the mind and then speak not to the ears of your partner but to her eyes, trying to get her to see what you see (*images*).
19. Alter your own tendencies (physical and vocal) to suit those of the character, particularly your sense of time and intensity of experience (tempo-rhythm), so none of your inappropriate mannerisms are imposed on the role (*external adjustments*).
20. Allow yourself to use all the previous research to free your entry into the heightened reality that allows you to both discover and control simultaneously (*creative mood*).

If one had to summarize the whole Stanislavski approach in one word, the best choice would be *empathy.* You empathize with someone when you so completely comprehend what that person is going through that you share her feelings, thoughts and motives. Empathy is a far more powerful connection than sympathy or pity. It generates an involuntary physical response beyond an intellectual/emotional one. You may watch a fight and actually feel a blow being struck with your whole being. Depending on which fighter you identify with, you may feel the blow received or the one given. This is empathy on the simplest level. You may also empathize to the degree that you can comprehend actions that most observers would find inhuman and beyond justification.

Contribution

Organized classes and degrees in acting were unknown when Stanislavski started working, so it might be argued that, without his contribution, your class might not even exist today. The System includes a close, careful look at the world of the character and then gradually enters the character's perspective. It is composed of objective means for taking on the subjective views of the character. It allows the actor to portray any person, however despicable at first glance, without judgment.

To Read More

Robert Barton, Chs. 4 Stanislavski's Sytem and 5 Stanislavski Stretched, *Acting Onstage and Off* (New York: Cengage Learning) 2015.
Konstantin Stanislavski (translated by Jean Benedetti), *An Actor's Work* (New York: Routledge) 2009.

10. Tadashi Suzuki (1939–)

Suzuki has made an impact on theatre by training actors who "can make the whole body speak even when one is silent."

Significance

In his stunning productions of Shakespeare and Greek tragedies, actors have shown awesome intensity, depth of feeling, grandeur and power rare on the contemporary stage. He shares with Bogart, his co-founder of the Saratoga Theatre Institute and frequent collaborator, a powerful belief that naturalistic acting is too limiting for the future. Suzuki is a much tougher taskmaster in his approach. (His classic and notorious inquiry to struggling actors in rehearsal: "Why you so bad?")

Key Ideas

He aspires to channel "animal energy" with a completely integrated expression of verbal and body language. He sees much of "modernized" theatre as a place of non-animal energy, including an over-reliance on technology, that has essentially "dismembered" us from our essential selves.

Whereas Bogart's Viewpoints focus on the acting ensemble as a single unit, Suzuki focuses on each actor's relationship to her own body. He has taken classical Japanese theatre and Indian Kathakali dancing and blended them with Western ballet. His training seeks an ideal form, an impossible perfection, the rewards being in the attempt. His forms require balance, stamina, strength and concentration for heightened theatricality and presence. One of the reasons his work is so powerful is that he has actors discover their characters' greatest desire and then magnify that desire many times over.

Suzuki's work always begins with feet as the root of expressivity (Michael Chekhov placed the same emphasis on feet and Meyerhold on the knees). There is a sense of grounding or what Suzuki calls "the attraction for the ground which the lower half of the body feels." Tremendous demands are placed on the lower body, while the upper body is often relaxed. His work honors the most ancient Japanese rituals of feet stomping to arouse energy and activate life, going back to the earliest Japanese stages, which were built on land where the dead were believed to dwell.

Suzuki classes are often accompanied by loud percussive music. While the music plays, actors are expected to fiercely beat the floor with their feet—then, when it stops, to relax, perhaps even to fall, and achieve complete quiet and stillness. The most vivid difference between his classes and most actor training is that, instead of relaxation and avoiding strain, he asks actors for mastery over strain. His work is an antidote to actors who tend to equate making small decisions inevitably with honest ones. He offers assistance in achieving huge moments of heightened expression and total commitment way beyond a prosaic, everyday believability.

Contribution

Bogart's and Suzuki's work has often been interwoven, so the best comparison of what they do comes from Bogart herself: "Suzuki training produces incredible concentration, focus, strength, and the ability to change quickly. Viewpoints deals with spontaneity and flexibility and being in the moment—it's a magic, chemical combination. The Suzuki is like a barre class for a dancer; Viewpoints is practicing creating fiction using time and space. One is vertical, the other is horizontal. One is you and God; the other is you and the people around you."

To Read More

Paul Allain, *The Art of Stillness: The Theater Practice of Tadashi Suzuki* (New York: Palgrave Macmillan) 2003.
Tadashi Suzuki, *The Way of Acting*, translated by J. Thomas Riner (New York: Theatre Communications Group) 1986.

11. Evgeni (Eugene) Vakhtangov (1883–1922)

Vakhtangov combined Stanislavski's inner technique with a vivid and exciting theatricalism and was dedicated to exploring the "grotesque." His short brilliant career ended when he died of cancer in 1922 at age 39, though supporters continued his work for many years at the Vakhtangov Theatre.

Significance

Though he was fond of exaggerated and distorted characters, all were based on inner truths. You could say he pushed the envelope on how large or eccentric a character could be and still have actors thrive by using a deep inner technique. He demonstrated that Stanislavski's System was entirely adaptable to styles far beyond realism.

Key Ideas

- *Adjustment:* Using motivations completely unrelated to the content of the play, secrets unconnected to the dramatic events and/or impulses that no one in the audience would recognize but would for the actor produce powerful emotion. For example, an actor playing a character avenging his mother's death might find asbestos or some other dangerous material in the dressing rooms and consider suing the theatre management, "avenging" all the actors who might be potential victims of management's carelessness. This is not what most actors consider "substitution" because the performer is not really attempting to find a parallel situation from his own life (an experience with his own mother or an actual murder) but rather an entirely different source of emotion.
- *Justification:* Finding reasons to come to the theatre that "justify" your participation in the play. For example, you are the one hope your character has to ever come alive again and be heard. In this case, putting yourself in the service of something higher may motivate you to a higher level of commitment. This moves the actor outside of self-preoccupation and the immediate needs of the character.

Contribution

Vakhtangov managed to employ the Stanislavski System into other periods and genres beyond contemporary realism, including classical theatre and highly "stylized" performance. He showed the System worked with numerous styles, including what he called "fantastic realism." He was profoundly influential on giving honest inner lives to characters in large, exaggerated circumstances. Vakhtangov influenced Richard Boleslavsky, who taught MAT techniques in New York and who in turn influenced Lee Strasberg.

To Read More

Andrei Malaev-Babel, *The Vakhtangov Sourcebook* (New York: Routledge) 2010.
Ruben Simonov, *Stanislavski's Protégé Eugene Vakhtangov*, translated and adapted by Miriam Goldina (New York: DBS, Inc.) 1969.

Disciplines

These areas of study are less associated with a single person. Some do have an important inventor, but that person's identity is less known than the name of the discipline itself. Some have existed in some form for so long that their origins are lost in the mists of time. They range from highly active to completely still, from individual initiative to giving up all action and allowing an expert to apply key pressure or touch. Many are integrated into acting programs or recommended for adjunct study. They offer a diverse spectrum of possible study.

1. Aikido

Aikido is a Japanese martial art developed by Morihei Ueshiba (1883–1969). The word "aikido" is formed of three logographic characters or kanji: *ai*—joining, unifying, combining, *ki*—spirit, energy, mood, morale, and *do*—way, path. Roughly translated as "the way of unifying life energy" or as "the way of harmonious spirit," it is a unique synthesis of martial arts, philosophy and spiritual beliefs. Sometimes called Osensei (Great Teacher), Ueshiba's goal was to create an art that practitioners could use to defend themselves while also protecting their attacker from injury.

Origins, Techniques

Ueshiba developed aikido after experiencing three instances of spiritual awakening: in 1925, 1940 and 1942. He created techniques consisting of entering and turning movements that redirect the momentum of an opponent's attack, and a throw or joint lock that terminates movement. Aikido focuses not on punching or kicking opponents, but rather on using their own energy to gain control of them or to throw them away from you. It is not a static art, but places great emphasis on motion and the dynamics of movement.

As Ueshiba grew older, more skilled and more spiritual in his outlook, his art became softer and more circular. Striking techniques became less important. In his own expression of the art there was a greater emphasis on what is referred to as *koky-nage*, or "breath throws," which are soft and blending, utilizing opponents' movement in order to throw them.

Practitioners claim to have found applicable self-defense techniques, spiritual enlightenment, physical health and/or peace of mind. Osensei emphasized the moral and holy aspects of this art, placing great weight on the development of harmony and peace.

Today aikido is found all over the world in a number of styles, with broad ranges of interpretation and emphasis. However, they all share techniques formulated by Ueshiba and most have concern for the well-being of the attacker.

Distinction

The blending of philosophical peace based beliefs with combat techniques, attacking with the idea of your opponent surviving.

Appeal

Many actors find the image of the Peaceful Warrior an appealing aspect of their physical regimens. Aikido can be an effective adjunct to stage combat training, where focus on the safety of your opponent is crucial.

To Read More

Mitusgi Saotome, *The Principles of Aikido* (Boston, MA: Shambhala) 1989.
Kisshōmaru Ueshiba, *The Art of Aikido: Principles and Essential Techniques* (Tokyo: Kodansha International) 2004.
Gaku Homma, *Aikido for Life* (Berkeley, CA: North Atlantic Books) 1990.

2. Alba Emoting

Alba Emoting (from Spanish roughly "White Portrayal") is a system for re-creating characteristics of strong, pure (or white) emotions through precise and technical methods.

Origins, Techniques

Neuroscientist Susana Bloch studied people experiencing the most powerful basic feelings (joy, sexual arousal, tenderness, grief, fear, anger) under hypnosis, using sophisticated equipment to monitor their breathing patterns, areas of muscle tension/relaxation, shifts in posture and gesture, and tendencies to make or avoid sound. The result is an accurate, systematic guide to how emotion is expressed. Her work shows that the "big" emotions are expressed identically among all the cultures.

Bloch found that emotions manifest through physical changes she calls "effector patterns." She isolated the universal characteristics of major states. For each emotion, she has determined the following:

1. a breathing pattern, characterized by amplitude and frequency modulation, and whether you inhale or exhale through the nose or mouth
2. a muscular activation characterized by a set of contracting or relaxing muscles, particularly those of the abdomen, and defined by a particular posture
3. facial muscle patterns forming particular expressions.

Bloch taught actors how to evoke emotional expression based on scientific evidence, from widely varying subjects. If something is missing in your portrayal of an emotion, a review of the Alba characteristics can often diagnostically enhance the believability of your portrayal.

For example, breathing patterns for laughing and crying are in exact opposition, even though both involve a gravitational force that gradually pulls one down to the ground. Crying involves inhalation invading exhalation, whereas in laughing it is exhalation invading inhalation, so the exact opposite phase of the breathing process dominates in each instance. When crying, we experience a twitching on the inhale and when laughing on the exhale; both can "bind up" the breathing pattern and result in a gasping for breath. All emotions except fear are centered in the abdomen, so concentrating on lowering the breath to that area can be an effective antidote to encroaching fear.

Distinction

Alba Emoting provides an amazingly effective blend of inner and outer technique. If you beckon emotion and it is not coming, reminding yourself of the breathing pattern and muscle tension of the feeling will make it very likely that the emotion will come and will also give you the power to present the characteristics—if you so choose—without letting the feeling overwhelm you. Alba Emoting combines science and art in a way that suggests phenomenal potential future collaborations as we learn more about how emotion happens.

Appeal

Anyone who has ever felt out of control or frightened when asked to produce powerful emotion in performance can benefit from it. So can anyone who has trouble producing believable laughter or tears onstage or anyone experiencing an "off night" and in need of some solid help.

To Read More

Roxane Rix, "Learning Alba Emoting," *Theatre Topics* 8.1 (March 1998).
Pamela Chabora, "The Method and Alba Emoting," *Method Acting Reconsidered*. Edited by
    David Krassner (New York: St. Martin's Press) 2000.

3. Chi Gung

Originating in China, Chi Gung or "Life Energy (chi) Cultivation (gung)" is a spiritual practice intended to align body, breath and mind for health, meditation and strength. Alternatively spelled QiGongor or Chi Kung, practice typically involves meditation, coordinating slow flowing movements, deep rhythmic breathing and a calm meditative state of mind. Chi Gung is practiced worldwide for recreation, exercise, relaxation and preventive medicine.

Origins, Techniques

Sometimes traced as far back as 2,000 years, it was taught largely in secret over centuries and outlawed during the Chinese Cultural Revolution of the 1960s. It was allowed to go public in 1976 with disparate approaches and widespread interest. Research has shown possible benefits for hypertension, pain and cancer treatment.

Chi, involving breath, air, gas and the relationship between matter, energy and spirit, is the central underlying principle in traditional Chinese medicine and martial arts. Gung, involving practice, skill, mastery, merit, service or result, is often used to mean a traditional sense of achievement through great effort. A wide variety of warm-ups and exercises are offered.

Distinction

Chi Gung differs from other similar forms in that the emphasis is constantly on the breath above all else and it is divided into two distinct forms: active (Dong Gung) which involves continuous movement and passive (Jing Gung) where the external body is still, either sitting or lying, while awareness is directed and felt in various body areas by breath or imagery or both. It also can involve treating a specific organ or area of pain and discomfort by directing chi to that area.

Appeal

Chi Gung offers particularly soothing ways of relaxing the mind, body and emotions, all useful to actors. It manifests vividly the admonition to remember to breathe deeply when under stress and can be practiced anywhere, including being in line or in a waiting room.

To Read More

K.S. Cohen, *The Way of Qigong: The Art and Science of Chinese Energy Healing* (New York: Random House of Canada) 1999.

Volker Scheid, *Chinese Medicine in Contemporary China: Plurality and Synthesis* (Durham, NC: Duke University) 2002.

4. Hakomi

Origins, Techniques

The Hakomi Method was created by psychotherapist Ron Kurtz (1934–2011). With a deep interest in systems theory, he integrated material derived from Taoist and Buddhist philosophy with the methods of somatic therapies of Bioenergetics, Feldenkrais and the process of psychotherapy. His approach regarded individuals as self-organizing systems influenced by core beliefs and memories that were expressed through attitudes and associated habits. The goal of Hakomi was to help people identify these patterns and transform those core beliefs that were not working for them into new belief systems.

Distinction

The Hakomi Method is an example of the many self-actualizing systems that evolved in the 1960s and 1970s. The goal of these methods was to help individuals achieve their full potential by an increased awareness of physical, psychological and emotional habits and providing methods that would allow for change. The primary ideas associated with the Hakomi Method are:

1. mindfulness or moment to moment awareness
2. nonviolent attitude toward self and other
3. unity of all experience
4. body–mind holism, an integration between the mind and the body.

Appeal

The Hakomi Method's appeal for the actor is in its sequencing of its process from establishing the attentiveness of mindfulness to the acknowledgment of the impact of core beliefs, to deepening an experience and related understanding of the belief system, to transformation through evolving a new scenario that is integrated into daily life.

To Read More

Ron Kurtz, *Body Centered Psychotherapy: The Hakomi Method* (New York: Life Rhythm) 1990.

Ron Kurtz, *The Body Reveals: How to Read Your Own Body* (New York: Harper Collins) 1984.

Halko Weiss and Greg Johanson, *Hakomi-Mindness Centered Somatic Psychotherapy: A Comprehensive Guide to Theory and Practice* (New York: W.W. Norton) 2015.

Geek meditation session.

Figure 3.3 Geek meditation session. Copyright Nitrozac and Snaggy.

5. Meditation

Origins, Techniques

Meditation is a practice in which one induces a mode of consciousness to self-regulate the mind, in order to promote relaxation, focus, energy and/or states of compassion and tolerance. Meditation has been practiced since antiquity as a component of numerous religious traditions and beliefs and is part of a variety of Asian physical disciplines. An ambitious form of meditation aims at effortlessly sustained single-pointed concentration, a component of Japanese Noh theatre.

The most widely practiced meditation forms in the U.S. are Mindfulness Meditation, based on principles of Buddhism, and TM or Transcendental Meditation, developed by Maharishi Mahseh Yogi in India in the mid-1950s. In the first, focus is intently on the breathing process. In the second, it is on the silent repetition of a mantra, chosen to distract the conscious mind while the unconscious works on greater states of peace. In most instances meditation is practiced sitting quietly with eyes closed.

Distinction

The importance for meditation in performance training is its application to stay present in the current moment by clearing and calming the mind and uniting it with internal states of the body/mind. The combination develops a psychophysical touch point that over time provides the focus concentration the actor needs to play major roles.

Appeal

Meditation and/or contemplative practices, particularly those that trace their lineage to Asian physical disciplines, are increasingly a component of actor training programs as they provide the knowledge of an individual's internal energy state in conjunction with an ability to project in performance this internal state externally.

And the value of a period of stillness and quiet cannot be overemphasized in conjunction with acting, an art potentially fraught with distraction and tension.

To Read More

Pema Chödrön, *How to Meditate: A Practice Guide to Making Friends with Your Mind* (New York: Sounds True) 2013.
Sharon Salzberg, *Real Happiness: The Power of Meditation* (New York: Workman) 2010.

6. NLP

Neuro Linguistic Programming (NLP) is a system that is often called "software for your brain" and focuses on how excellence can be transferred. It is about learning how others code information so you can connect with them better and learning to recode your own information process so you can function more effectively. It involves Neuro (brain and nervous system), Linguistic (language and nonverbal communication), Programming (shortcuts and codes). It offers a series of exercises for identifying and changing behavior and learning patterns.

Origins, Techniques

NLP started when two researchers (John Grinder and Richard Bandler) studied three legendary therapists (Virginia Satir, Milton Erickson and Fritz Perls), asking, "What do brilliant communicators do that can be taught to others?" It is now taught at more than 100 institutes in the United States and a similar number throughout the rest of the world. NLP has significantly affected therapy, business, law and early childhood and elementary education. It is new to theatre but offers strikingly original processes for the training of actors.

Distinction

The part of NLP that is best known is the idea of determining whether you are primarily a visual (V), auditory (A) or kinesthetic (K) learner.

1. Do you like to study using lists and outlines? Do you use words such as *see*, *shows*, *focus*, *perspective*, *looks*? Are you straight-backed, even when sitting, with raised, tense shoulders, a dropped chin, minimal facial expression and few gestures? Is your speech rapid, breathy, high-pitched, uninflected? You may be visual.

2. Do you like to study and run lines with others, having them ask you questions and hearing yourself answer? Do you favor phrases such as *tell myself*, *rings a bell*, *I hear you*? Do you like to sit when talking, touch your own face, tap out rhythms, and sometimes turn your ears toward others when they speak to you? Do you really like to talk, nod often when listening, and sometimes repeat exactly what you've been asked before answering? Is your voice pleasant and your speech varied? You are auditory.

3. Do you have trouble studying? Do you need to get up and pace and do things to take in information? Would you always build a model rather than write a paper if you had a choice? Do you say *grasp*, *handle*, *feel* and other similarly physical verbs? Do you need space, gesture big and often, like to be up acting out experiences and feelings, but slump when sitting? Are you highly expressive and emotionally available but also sometimes lose the thread of a speaker's (or your own) main points, so you alternate between energized and comatose? You're a kino.

Most of us (actors in particular) shift between modes as our experiences vary. As soon as you know yourself and recognize others, you raise your capacity to connect positively. A visual-learner acting teacher may correct a kinesthetic actor on the pronunciation of a word a thousand times, explaining how it is spelled (because she "sees" the word) over and over. Once she recognizes the actor is a kino, who will only pronounce the word differently if she explains how it *feels* to move the lips, teeth and tongue into the correct pronunciation, the actor pronounces the word right, and the teacher no longer wants to kill him. This tension could also exist between you and your scene partner and any other working combination.

A visual actor will wish to highlight his script and return to looking at the words frequently during rehearsal. An auditory actor may wish to record and play back often. A kinesthetic needs to get into the right shoes and rehearsal garments and start using props and making contact with others at the earliest possible moment. An outstanding actor will work to access learning modes he does not habitually employ so that he can join any partner.

Appeal

NLP has the potential to assist the whole acting process: greatly reducing performance anxiety, helping actors communicate more clearly, intensifying character analysis, stimulating imaginative rehearsal choices and helping everyone involved in a project to let go when the time comes for it to end.

> *NLP is the most powerful vehicle for change in existence.*
> **Psychology Today**

To Read More

Robert Barton, *Acting Reframes* (New York: Routledge) 2011.
Anne Linden, *Mindworks: An Introduction to N.L.P.* (Bethel, CT: Crown House Publishing) 2008.
Joseph O'Connor and John Seymour, *Introducing N.L.P.* (London: Aquarian Press) 1990.

7. Reflexology

Reflexology is the application of appropriate pressure to specific points and areas on the feet, hands or ears in the belief that these areas and reflex points correspond to different body organs and systems, and that pressing them has a beneficial effect on the organs and person's general health. It is based on a system of zones and reflexes.

A unifying theme is the idea that areas on the foot correspond to areas of the body, and that by manipulating these one can improve health through one's chi. For example, reflexology holds that a specific spot in the arch of the foot corresponds to the bladder point. When a reflexology practitioner uses thumbs or fingers to apply appropriate pressure to this area, it affects bladder functioning. Reflexologists divide the body into ten equal vertical zones, five on the right and five on the left.

Origins, Techniques

Practices resembling reflexology have been documented in the ancient histories of China and Egypt. Reflexology was introduced to the United States in 1913 by Willaim H. Fitzgerald M.D. (1872–1942), an ear, nose and throat specialist, and Dr. Edwin Bowers. It was modified in the 1930s and 1940s by Eunice D. Ingham (1889–1974), a nurse and physiotherapist. Ingham claimed that the feet and hands were especially sensitive, and mapped the entire body into "reflexes" on the feet, renaming "zone therapy" as reflexology. Modern reflexologists use Ingham's methods or similar techniques developed by the reflexologist Laura Norman.

Distinction

While most forms of physical therapy target areas of anatomy directly, reflexology is unique in contacting areas via another area of the body altogether. It has proven popular when used not exclusively, but as an adjunct to other treatments.

Appeal

The process is considered pleasant and while there is no solid scientific evidence, participants frequently report greater personal satisfaction, less stress and improved health.

To Read More

Kevin Kunz and Barbara Kunz, *The Complete Guide to Foot Reflexology* (New York: Reflexology Research Project) 1993.

Laura Norman and Thomas Cowan, *The Reflexology Handbook: A Complete Guide*, (New York: Piatkus) 1989.

8. Rolfing

Origins, Techniques

Ida P. Rolf's (1896–1979) initial interest in the 1930s was the body's relationship to gravity and the theories and techniques of osteopathy and yoga. She expanded her understanding through her work with members of the Esalen Institute in California, including psychologists such as Fritz Perls who were interested in the concept of human potential. In 1971 she founded the Rolf Institute of Structural Integration.

Distinction

The primary goal of Rolfing is to improve the alignment and movement of the body. Ida P. Rolf theorized that the fascia (connective tissues) restricted muscles from ease of function and that the separation of the bound up fascia manually released tension built up in the body. Unlike other human potential methods, Rolfing incorporates the hands on manipulation of the fascia which surrounds all body organs and muscles. It is typically performed in a progression of ten sessions in which the Rolfer manipulates the fascia until they believe they are operating in conjunction with the muscles in a more optimal relationship.

Appeal

Many actors have discovered that the Rolfing sessions have helped them reorganize their bony and muscular structure to provide a greater ease of movement and a more integrated alignment. This has meant they have more energy for demanding stage roles and the creation of detailed physical characters.

To Read More

Ida P. Rolf, *The Integration of Human Structures* (New York: Harper Collins) 1978.
Ida P. Rolf, *Rolfing and Physical Reality* (New York: Healing Arts Press) 1990.

9. Shiatsu

Shiatsu is a form of Japanese bodywork based on traditional Chinese medical theories. Shiatsu means "finger pressure." The aim of shiatsu is to restore the proper flow of bodily energy by massaging the surface of the skin along the meridian lines.

Origins, Techniques

Shiatsu evolved from *anma*, a Japanese massage modality developed in 1320 by Akashi Kan Ichi. Anma was popularized in the seventeenth century by acupuncturist Sugiyama Waichi. Around the same time the first books on the subject, including Fujibayashi Ryohaku's *Anma Tebiki* (Manual of Anma), appeared. The Fujibayashi school carried anma into the modern age. Tokurjiro Namikoshi (1905–2000) founded his shiatsu college in the 1940s and is often credited with inventing modern shiatsu. His legacy was the state recognition of shiatsu as an independent method of treatment in Japan. Namikoshi's school taught shiatsu within a framework of Western medical science. A student and teacher of this school, Shizuto Masunga, brought shiatsu back to a traditional Eastern medicine and philosophic framework. He founded Zen Shiatsu.

Techniques include massages with fingers, thumbs and palms, assisted stretching, joint manipulation and mobilization. To examine a patient, a shiatsu practitioner uses palpation (exploration with hands) and sometimes pulse diagnosis.

Distinction

Shiatsu is one of the few forms of physical therapy in which almost everything, from examination to diagnosis to various treatments, is done through the hands of the expert practitioner, though occasionally elbows and knees may be employed. It has sometimes been described as needle free acupuncture. Pressure may also be applied to any of the 600 or so acupoints which are located just under the skin along the meridians, tiny energy structures that affect the flow of chi through the body.

Appeal

Proponents claim increased relaxation, improved digestion, reduction in back pain and headaches, anxiety, insomnia, fatigue and arthritis pain, and rapid recovery from injuries. It is considered holistic in treating the entire body over specific areas of complaint.

To Read More

Chris Jarmey and Gabriel Mojay, *Shiatsu: The Complete Guide* (London: Thorsons) 1991.
Allan R. Cook, *Alternative Medicine Sourcebook* (Detroit, MI: Omnigraphics) 1999.

10. T'ai Chi

T'ai chi ch'uan, which literally translates as "supreme or boundless fist" or "great extremes boxing," is an internal Chinese martial art practiced for both its defense training and its health benefits, but increasingly for the latter exclusively. A more common contemporary translation is "supreme ultimate health exercises." It is perhaps the most popular exercise practiced today, with estimates that up to 20 percent of the world's population are practitioners.

"I must warn you, I know tai chi. We can step outside and settle it like men, but it will have to be in slow motion."

Figure 3.4 Manly t'ai chi. Copyright Mike Baldwin.

Origins, Techniques

Formative influences are traced to Taoist and Buddhist monasteries as far back as 1200 years. Choy Hok Pang was the first known proponent of t'ai chi to openly teach in the United States in 1939. Sophia Delza, a professional dancer, performed the first known public demonstration of t'ai chi ch'uan in the U.S. at the Museum of Modern Art in 1954 and also wrote the first English language book on the subject, *T'ai Chi Ch'uan: Body and Mind in Harmony*, in 1961.

There are five major styles of t'ai chi, each named after the Chinese family from which it originated. Training involves five elements: taolu (solo hand and weapons routines/forms), neigong and gigong (breathing, movement and awareness exercises and meditation), tuishou (response drills) and sanshou (self-defense techniques).

Distinction

T'ai chi is typically engaged with very slow movements. The physical techniques are characterized by the use of leverage through the joints based on coordination and relaxation, rather than muscular tension, in order to neutralize, yield or initiate attacks. The slow, repetitive work involved in the process of learning how that leverage is generated gently and measurably increases, opens internal circulation. Exercises are simple, yet sophisticated, and encourage muscles to let go of tension, the mind to let go of worry and the heart to let go of angst. Participants move through a series of choreographed slow motion martial arts movements in a state of absolute relaxation. Sometimes called an "innercise," it works body and mind simultaneously, and proponents claim it releases them from grudges, prejudices and other distractions that keep us tied to the past.

Appeal

As much as any activity in this chapter, t'ai chi has found popularity with people from all walks of life who report profound relief from tension and a great sense of peace. Because the actions are done upright, it can be practiced almost anyplace, anytime with no particular necessary clothing, by almost anyone, including those in wheel chairs.

To Read More

Tsung-Hwa Jou, *Tao of T'ai Chi Chuan*, 3rd ed. (Singapore: Tuttle) 1998.
Kam Man Choy, *Tai Chi Chuan* (San Francisco, CA: Memorial Edition) 1994.

11. Visualization

Visualization is the technique of utilizing one's imagination to visualize particular behaviors or events occurring in one's life. Practitioners create a detailed schema of what they desire and then visualize it repeatedly with all of the senses.

Origins, Techniques

Visualization practices are a common form of spiritual exercise. In Vajrayan Buddhism, complex visualizations have long been used to attain the Buddahood state of enlightenment. Visualization is also used extensively in sports psychology. The process, sometimes referred to as creative visualization, became part of the human potential movement in the 1960s and 1970s, with the goal of using focused concentration with an image to resolve issues associated with life habits.

Distinction

Creative visualization's focus on the future distinguishes it from numerous passive activities that are about being in the present moment. However, present visualization is also a component of some forms of meditation with a focus on the breath, a sound, a phrase or an image.

Appeal

People from highly varying backgrounds have practiced creative visualization as a successful approach to enhance execution, improve aptitudes and support trust. Actors are often drawn to employing many of the same techniques used by athletes, but adapting them to envision success in auditions and other high pressure performance conditions.

To Read More

Kevin Anderson, *Visualization* (Pittsburgh, PA: Creative Space Publishing) 2015.
Angel Mendez, *Creative Visualization* (Pittsburgh, PA: Creative Space Publishing) 2014.
Jack Moore, *Visualization Manifesto* (Raleigh, NC: Lulu Press) 2014.

12. *Yoga*

Yoga is a Hindu spiritual and ascetic discipline, a part of which, including breath control, simple meditation, stretching and the adoption of specific bodily postures, is widely practiced for health and relaxation. The word "yoga" comes from the Sanskrit *root yuj*, which means "to join" or "to yoke."

Origins, Techniques

There is no consensus on the chronology or specific origin of yoga. The origins of yoga have been speculated to date back to pre-Vedic Indian traditions, but most likely developed around 5,000 years ago, in ancient India's ascetic circles. Modern yoga is based on five principles created by Swami Sivananda: proper relaxation, exercises, breathing, diet and thinking. There are many branches of yoga, but in the West yoga largely refers to Hatha yoga, i.e. the physical postures (yoga asanas) and yogic breathing techniques (pranayama), which are the main focus of most people's yoga practice. The yoga postures and yoga breathing techniques of Hatha yoga purify and strengthen the body to increase the flow of vital energy, or prana, and still the constant chatter of the mind.

Yoga postures are believed to help increase body awareness, and therefore offer a welcome alternative to the mindless, repetitive movements of many workout styles.

Distinction

Unlike the continuous motion characterizing many Asian disciplines, yoga involves a series of relatively static poses and slow stretches, and numerous positions are done lying down. It is completely noncompetitive and allows all participants to move at their own rate, though recently there has been a rise in Vanyasa and Bikrem Yoga where movement from pose to pose is quite rapid.

Appeal

Yoga exercises, in part because of the effective stretching or more accurately lengthening they offer, have made their way into numerous basic acting warm-ups. Yoga is very user-friendly; the strengthening effects of yoga asanas are achieved gently and gradually, without pushing or forcing. It has been adapted for highly varying participants.

To Read More

M.E. Dahkid, *Yoga: The Essential Guide* (M.E. Dahkid: Draft2Digital) 2015.
T.K.V. Desikachar, *The Heart of Yoga* (Rochester, VT: Inner Traditions Yoga) 1999.

Summary

In this chapter, we have established the need for effective movement training to be somatic. We have identified the most prominent contributors to training as well as additional widely practiced disciplines. What distinguishes each endeavor has been established as well as its importance. You now have some familiarity with areas of study that could be part of your department's training program and some basics on which to choose among many options for your individual regimen.

CHAPTER 4 EVOLVING MOVEMENT

Evolving Movement

Developing psychophysical movement methods suited to all theatre forms

Each phase of a movement, every small transference of weight, every single gesture of any part of the body reveals some feature of our inner life.

Rudolf von Laban, acting innovator

Energy

Constantin Stanislavski describes energy as flowing "down the network of your muscular system, arousing your inner motor centers and stirring you to external activity." As he notes, the quality of this energy is revealed in physical actions:

> *Energy, heated by emotion, charged with will, directed by the intellect, moves with confidence and pride, like an ambassador on an important mission. It manifests itself in conscious action, full of feeling, content and purpose, which cannot be carried out in any slipshod, mechanical way, but must be fulfilled in accordance with its spiritual impulses.*

All physical methods claim the self as inseparable from the body and involve learning to listen and live inside your sensations and related deep internal connections. The ultimate goal of increased physical awareness is being in the present moment, which provides the opportunity to note previous habits and transform them into new skills and competencies.

You learned in formative years the appropriate physical displays for a variety of social situations, from the visit of a favorite relative to ritual events such as weddings and funerals. You bring physical tendencies to move certain ways based on your sensory memories of what is culturally appropriate. Your posture sets the tone of the interaction, while your gestures express your desires. The merging of posture and gesture is your psychological life made visible.

Figure 4.1 Rudolf von Laban's influence on movement for actors has been profound, with numerous highly original ways of framing physical actions.

Your physical actions can be described by body part used (as in arms, legs and head), the direction in space the body takes (forward, back, diagonal) and the general movement shape (symmetrical, asymmetrical). However, movement can also be described in terms of its primary dynamic, an approach based on the movement research of Rudolf von Laban, an innovator noted in Chapter 3. We believe that Laban's concepts are invaluable to your growth in terms of movement awareness. They are also the basis for the development of the physical life of a character.

Born in 1879 in the Austro-Hungarian Empire, Laban had the opportunity to observe people in diverse environments because his father, an army officer, was stationed in various parts of Europe and the Middle East. He studied art and dance in Paris, started a dance community that initiated a series of art festivals until the outbreak of World War I, then moved to Zurich, where he developed a method for analyzing movement. Between world wars, he established dance schools in several European countries, created a choreographic institute, directed pageants and became director of the Allied State Theatres in Germany. His work was banned in 1935 by the Nazi party as not sufficiently nationalist. Subsequently, he moved to Manchester, England, where he published a series of books outlining his methods of movement analysis, education and notation.

Laban's Efforts

Through observing and analyzing individual movement, Laban discovered most people have *energetic qualities* which are the result of interaction with the social/cultural environment. These largely unconscious gestural styles interact through the neuromuscular system to generate physical choices that fall into the range of what Laban termed *effort*.

"Effort" is the term used to refer to the inner urge or drive towards movement. The result will be either an action (a gesture, step, body shift, working action) if fully developed, or, in one initiated which then dies away, a "shadow movement" (a small body movement, seemingly, with no external aim; a raised eyebrow or frown, a tapping finger, a shoulder twitch, a fleeting look of recognition).

Rudolf von Laban

When people interact, they commit to a set of actions that usually take a particular attitude or tendency toward one or more of these efforts. Laban divided the energy shapes into four categories: *flow*, *weight*, *time* and *space*. Each category is subdivided into two opposites that represent a continuum:

1. flow—bound to free
2. weight—strong to light
3. time—sudden to sustained
4. space—direct to indirect.

Individual movement styles create a *movement signature* that is a combination of different efforts such as sustained (time) and bound (flow), for example, or sudden (time) and direct (space). Learning to distinguish visually and kinesthetically the various efforts will increase your potential choices by expanding your range of movement. Understanding the efforts also provides a method for analyzing the movement of others.

Laban's explorations begin by discovering the general state of the body for each quality and its related continuum. He distinguishes between physical states that release into the forces of gravity, referred to as indulgent, and physical states that resist gravity's forces, called resistant. Indulgent qualities are free, sustained, light and indirect. Resisting qualities are strong, bound, sudden and direct.

We can do every imaginable movement and then select those that are the most suitable and desirable for our own nature. These can be found only by each individual. For this reason, practice of the free use of kinetic and dynamic possibilities is of the greatest advantage. We should be acquainted both with the general movement capacities of a healthy body and mind and with the specific restrictions and capacities resulting from the individual structure of our own bodies and minds.

Rudolf von Laban

Flow

Flow refers to the manner in which we manage our movement. It can be either *successive* or *simultaneous*. Successive (or sequential) is a series of continuous movement from one body part to another. Simultaneous involves moving all body parts at the same time to accomplish a physical task. For example, when walking across the floor, your body moves in a sequence of gestures initiated in the hips, knees or feet. A walk is a successive movement. If it were obviously simultaneous, the entire leg from hip to toe would move as a unit. A sequential movement through you, either from your head to your feet or the reverse, is analogous to a body wave. There can also be waves of individual limbs and from limb to torso.

Free flow is a movement difficult to stop suddenly. The flow of energy projects itself through you with no specific target. Words used to describe free flow are: fluid, uncontrolled, abandoned and wholehearted.

Bound flow involves stopping or inhibiting the flow of movement. On the continuum of free to bound, there is movement that is beyond stopping—like someone tumbling over a cliff—and there is movement that is absolutely held—like holding your breath. Between these two extremes are states in which muscles are in various states of contraction. Related words used to describe bound are: careful, controlled, restrained and cautious.

Whether you move the entire body at once (simultaneous) or as a sequence of parts (successive/sequential), you are managing your flow of energy. You are literally "feeling" the situation and deciding how to act as you interpret the moment. The exercises in this section begin and end in neutral. Please refer to Chapter 2 for a review of the use of breath and focus that are part of neutral.

EXERCISE 4.1 **FLOW–FREE TO BOUND**

1. Begin in neutral. Start walking around the room, imagining you are on the beach, an entire week of sun and relaxation in front of you, absolutely free of responsibility. The very idea of having no immediate tasks makes you begin to play on the beach like a three-year-old, running toward the waves, throwing sand against the wind, and chasing sand flies.
2. Suddenly all your muscles contract at the same time. You find it difficult to move. It is as if you have become a dense mass.
3. You concentrate on releasing the muscles of your upper torso, arms and right leg, but the left leg still feels like a mass of clay.
4. Now, as if your body were playing tricks on you, your right leg seems to have become clay, but your left leg moves freely.
5. You keep moving around, trying to change the feeling of your leg by walking around, sitting, lying down and standing again. You notice that the "clay" feeling has finally left your legs, but now your hips feel like clay.

   Finally, you begin running up and down the beach in desperation, jiggling each part of your body until you are able to recapture that sense of physical freedom you had when you first started playing on the beach.

6. Return to neutral.
7. How would you describe your physical embodiment of bound flow? Free flow?

EXERCISE 4.2 **FLOW VARIATIONS**

1. Create any task—for example, putting on or taking off articles of clothing (coat, hat, shoes).
2. Perform the task in a state of successive flow. Find moments in the task when the flow is free. When the flow is bound. Experiment with various combinations of bound to free or free to bound. What happens to your breath in each state?
3. Each exploration develops new levels of awareness through the different qualities on the effort continuum. When working with the qualities, you will want to expand your ability to work from physical metaphor by noting your reactions to your experience of each quality. What are the words and phrases that come to mind when you begin moving in the quality? How would you complete the following sentence? I move like_____; I feel like_____; I respond to the world by interacting like _____; I sound like_____.

Weight

Your relationship to gravity can be either *strong* or *light* and tells you "who" you are with regards to the pull of the earth. Are you resisting gravity, releasing into it, or negotiating with it? Your experience of gravity extends into your communication style and interactions. A *strong* movement causes a forceful exertion in a particular direction. This exertion can be in response to a single physical choice such as a strong gesture with any body part exerting itself against gravity. It can also be a response to an outside kinetic force moving a body or body parts forcefully. Strong static force results from internal counter tensions, producing a firm, braced condition as either pushing or pulling. In each case, the kinesthetic system is working at a level of contraction that varies in intensity. Strong interaction with resistance from outside is met with resistance from the inside. There is a narrowing of your body's focus in a specific direction. Words used to describe strong are: resist, force, defy, oppose and prevent.

A *light* movement requires minimal force or tension and counter tension. A light exertion of the muscles away from gravity keeps the body off the floor sufficiently and prevents the skeletal system from slumping almost as if you were a filled balloon. Light interaction with outside force means limited resistance such as a slight touch, a gentle push, a delicate contact, with subtle and sensitive tension. Light actions convey the feeling of being carried by the air. Activation in the center of the torso (chest, sternum, ribs and upper back) along with support from the lower trunk provides optimal conditions for producing lightness. Words used to describe light are: tame, subdue, calm, pacify and placate.

The weight continuum defines the individual style of the action or the personality of a character. The form of a gesture and its relationship to gravity express the character's position regarding the emotional and physical balance of a social situation.

EXERCISE 4.3 **WEIGHT–STRONG TO LIGHT**

STRONG:

1. Begin by lying on the floor in a neutral state.
2. Imagine you are being held to the earth by some invisible force that prevents you from standing.
3. Commit all your strength to the physical action of trying to get up from the ground. Each time you start to get free you are pulled back to the ground by a force stronger than yourself. Initiate your attempts with different parts of your body—your hands, legs, torso, head. Note how you are using the breath as you resist the force.
4. Finally, you manage to pull yourself to upright and walk around the room, aware that the force that was holding you still has a grip on your feet.
5. Walking, you are aware of moving to defy or combat, oppose, resist the force that would pull you down.
6. Release your walk of resistance and return to your normal walk. Note how the walk that was resisting, opposing, defying and combating the force is different from your normal walking. Continue walking but stop suddenly where the force that is in the ground emerges in front of you.
7. Find a stance to oppose this force, which has now moved closer to your side, although you continue to resist its pressure.
8. The force keeps changing position and is trying to pull you to itself. Defy the force by committing your entire self to resisting and escaping it. This may mean that you need to pull, push or thrust the force away from you. This may put you into a mode of running away from the force. Run, feeling the force behind you trying to pull you to itself, first from one direction and then from another.
9. Return to neutral.
10. Lie back down on the floor.
11. Get up and note how much effort it took to get up.
12. Lie down again.

LIGHT:

13. Begin in neutral. Imagine yourself as a deflated person-balloon similar to those in parades.
14. Feel yourself being inflated as the balloon fills from the feet upward. First your feet fill with air, followed by your calves, thighs, hips, pelvis, rib cage, shoulders, head, arms and hands. As you become more and more filled with air, note that you have a desire to rise and move around the room. The only thing holding you to the floor is a set of strings tied at your ankles, knees, hips, wrists, elbows and top of the head.
15. See someone come and snip the strings that are attaching you at your head, wrists and elbows to the ground. As they cut the strings, your upper body begins to float upward.

16. See someone come and snip the strings that are keeping your hips, knees and ankles connected to the floor. As they snip these strings, you slowly come to an upright position.

17. Begin to float around the room. As you float, become aware of the gentle breezes that calmly push you one way and then another, maybe even delicately lifting you off the floor.

18. Finally, a slow leak develops in your balloon and you glide gently back to the floor.

19. Come to standing.

20. Using your kinesthetic memory and the physical organization for both strong and light, move around the room going from walking to running, jumping, leaping, hopping, turning. How do you organize yourself differently for a strong run and a light run? A strong hop and a light hop? A strong leap and a light leap? A strong jump and a light jump? A strong turn and a light turn? If you had to describe a strong run, what adjectives would you use? Light run? Strong hop? Light hop? Strong leap? Light leap? Strong jump? Light jump? What breath phrasing are you using with each? How can you use the breath to more specifically embody strength? Lightness?

21. Return to neutral.

22. What possible situations would create an experience of resistance to and/or release into gravity? Create an improvisation using one of these situations.

How would you describe your physical embodiment of strong? Light?

Time

Time refers to the *duration* of a movement. Sudden is a fast movement of short duration and corresponding acceleration. Sudden has a moment of stillness and then a burst of energy. Sudden can be felt as an immediate discharge of kinetic energy. Sudden gestures can continue after you have stopped moving and are experienced as feelings of urgency which may include vibrations such as shivering. Words used to describe sudden are: urgent, sharp and excited.

Sustained is a slow movement of a longer duration and longer deceleration, during which you have a sense of expanding into space. Sustained is a constant loop of transformation. It can be felt as a gradual change from one situation to another or as an unhurried departure. Words used to describe sustained are: prolonged, legato, indulgent and lingering.

Time dictates the "when" of any action, indicating the style of your reaction to other people and events. Are you slow or quick to respond? As a consequence, do you seem aggressive or passive in your stance toward others?

EXERCISE 4.4 **TIME–SUSTAINED TO SUDDEN**

SUSTAINED:

1. Begin in neutral with feet parallel, knees comfortably bent. You should be supported in the lower abdomen with the tail bone dropped toward the floor. Breathe in and out from the lower abdomen, sending the breath out through your head, the palms of your hands and the soles of your feet.
2. Inhale, allowing yourself to rise until you are balanced on your toes.
3. Exhale, sinking until your knees are slightly bent, heels flat on the floor.
4. Once this pattern is established, start moving around the room, keeping the sense of rising and lowering in extended, continuous time. Allow your arms to replicate the phrasing of the legs and torso, reaching out into space as you exhale and releasing in toward the body as you inhale.
5. Maintaining the relationship with the breath, reach into space with head, hands, shoulders, feet, knees, hips, back, elbows. It may feel as though you are under water. Keep the continuous nature of the movement that seemingly has no distinct beginning or end.
6. Move at different speeds and still maintain the same quality. Ask yourself: How do I initiate the movement? Once I begin to explore the quality, what is its relationship to the breath? Do I work within any specific breathing pattern?
7. Finally, reduce the movement to a walk.
8. Observe how you organize your body around this sense of time. What do you note about the relationship between your pelvis, spine, legs, arms, head?
9. Return to neutral.

SUDDEN:

10. Begin in neutral. Imagine that you are walking down a busy street and a small boy runs out into the street.
11. Quickly chase after him, dodging several moving cars to prevent getting hit yourself. Get to the boy, snatch him up and then return to the sidewalk, again dodging all the cars.
12. Return to your normal walk.
13. Imagine you are walking along a trail in a dense forest at twilight. You are enjoying the beauty of the trees when an arrow hits a tree next to you.
14. Startled, you start running.
15. While running, you discover several people chasing you and you must propel yourself around a series of trees and boulders up ahead.
16. You manage to negotiate the obstacles and get to a clearing, but now your pursuers have almost caught up to you.
17. They begin shooting arrows at your feet and other parts of your body. The only way you can prevent yourself from getting hurt is to move quickly out of the way, first one body part and then another, sometimes even your entire body.

18. Return to normal walk.
19. Remembering the kinesthetic qualities of sustainment, try walking, running, leaping, jumping, falling, skipping with sustainment. What adjectives would you use to describe each?
20. Return to your normal walk. Remember the physical state of suddenness. Investigate the other possibilities of this time quality through the movements mentioned above. What words would you use to describe each?
21. Return to your normal walk. Allow this walk to be transformed into a stride as you walk around the room. Change this to stalking, creeping, crawling. What flow, weight and time qualities are contained in each of the above? What possible situations might cause you to move in such a manner?
22. Return to your normal walk.
23. Allow this walk to be transformed into a dart, a dash, a sprint, a bolt. Repeat, moving back and forth between each. What qualities are contained in each of the above? How are you engaging your breath with each? What situations might call for you to move in such a manner?
24. Return to your normal walk.
25. Allow the walk to be transformed into a run and begin to flee, to avoid, to evade some person, mechanical being, animal. What qualities are contained in each? What situations might call for you to move in such a manner?
26. Return to your normal walk.
27. Allow the walk to be transformed into drifting through the room. Allow this walk to evolve into an object or animal that glides, that floats. What qualities of movement are contained in each experience? What situations might call for you to move in such a manner?
28. Return to neutral.

How would you describe your embodiment of sustained? Sudden?

Space

When you physically negotiate your way through different environments and social situations, you are spatially considering your next action, continually incorporating degrees of *direct* or *indirect* qualities. *Direct* is keeping strictly to the path or to the point; as such, narrowing your focus. Attention is kept directly on the place of arrival or key points passed through; the space on either side of the pathway of the action has no importance. Words or phrases used to describe direct are: pinpointed, channeled, zeroing in, single focus and restricted use of space.

Indirect/flexible is a movement that wanders, several parts of the body going in different directions simultaneously as the energy is not specific in terms of direction. Indirect always leaves an opportunity for something else to happen. As a personality characteristic, it appears as a slight hesitancy. Words used to describe indirect/flexible are: roundabout, wavy and undulating.

The body's focus shifts continuously. Walking in a dark room, unable to see, might require a sudden indirect focus. Often, but not always, direct movement reads as serious confidence and indirect as comedic hesitancy. Spatial choices also indicate your relationships to others and may overlap. If you find yourself in a rough neighborhood, you may avoid contact with others (indirect) while focusing strongly on getting out of there (direct).

EXERCISE 4.5 **SPACE–DIRECT TO INDIRECT**

1. Begin in neutral and start walking around the room using your normal walk. Explore each of the following scenarios as separate experiences.
2. Take a direct path that uses right angles. You can move sideways, forward and backward, but keep your focus forward. How do you integrate your breath into the decision to change directions? Stop. Now just walk around the room taking any path you want, but do not bump into any person or object.
3. Extend the action of walking to an imaginary game of basketball. See yourself surrounded by other players who want to take the ball away from you. To keep the ball you have to constantly and unexpectedly change your path in relationship to the other players. This causes you to constantly change focus and direction.
4. Imagine you are encased in a giant, invisible bubble of some unknown material. Reach out and touch the edges of the bubble with various body parts. With the sides of your arms. Investigate the bubble with your feet. With the sides of your torso. Continue the investigation of the dimensions of the bubble with your head, the sides of your legs. Note the ways you are organizing your body to explore the dimensions and texture of the bubble. Where is your breath in relationship to your point of stillness? What is your kinesthetic image related to this point?
5. An imaginary mosquito lands on your nose and then flies away. It returns to land on another part of your body and moves away. You decide to get it. Try to follow the movement of the mosquito with your eyes. Try to catch the mosquito with one hand. Try both hands.
6. An imaginary snake begins to crawl in front of you. You decide to stamp on it with your foot but it keeps moving. You keep trying to step on it but it moves one way and another. You keep trying to follow its movements by guessing which way it will go next. You cannot seem to judge enough in advance, and the snake finally slithers off. What happened to your breath during this scenario?
7. Return to a normal walk, move from direct to indirect. Allow any part of yourself to initiate the change in direction. If you were going to describe moving indirectly, what words would you use? What would they be for direct?
8. Return to neutral.

How would you describe your embodiment of direct? Indirect?

Laban's Effort Actions

The first section of this chapter has helped expand your understanding of different efforts, their relationship to your movement preferences, and the possibility of using them to extend your physical imagination, often consisting of two or more in combination. Laban organized possible effort combinations into what he referred to as the *eight basic actions* that are an indication of an individual's psychology and personality:

> *Weight, Space, Time, and Flow are the motion factors toward which the moving person adopts a definite attitude. These attitudes can be described as: relaxed or forceful toward weight, pliant or lineal toward space, prolonging or shortening toward time, and liberating or withholding attitude toward flow.*

When a quick response is needed in order to have a situation resolved immediately, actions include:

    a direct and strong punch
    an indirect/flexible and strong slash
    a direct and light dab
    an indirect/flexible and light flick

A slower response is guided by hesitation or a decision to delay. This may involve a direct and strong press and a flexible and strong wring. Actions associated with less resistance include:

    a direct and light glide
    an indirect/flexible and light float
    a direct and sustained press
    an indirect and sustained wring

The following explorations help you to research these actions.

Thrusting and Slashing

Thrusting is sudden, strong and direct. The action is one that moves in a straight line away from you, toward an opponent's body or to a specific destination, and may involve stamping and punching gestures.

Slashing is sudden, strong and indirect. It moves flexibly through space, causing you to leap and twist, sometimes turning and slashing in one direction, then immediately in another.

Gliding and Floating

Gliding is sustained, light and direct. Gliding movements are without undulations or curves and involve moving through space with a clearly determined goal, as in glide like a skater, glide like an airplane or glide like a skateboard.

Floating is also sustained and light, but it is indirect instead of direct. It often moves from the wrist, fingers and elbows to take you indirectly about the space. The legs lift lightly off the floor in careful rising and falling steps, as in float like a boat, a balloon or a cloud.

Wringing and Pressing

Wringing is sustained, strong and indirect. This form of gesture creates twisting, wrenching movements that knot in and open out as in wringing out a heavy wet towel. Initiate such movement by twisting one limb first in one direction and then another. Complete the same gesture with each limb, followed by various body parts in combination, exploring the combination of gestures that are sustained, strong and indirect.

Pressing is sustained, strong and direct. It involves pressing away from the body into space, and may involve resistance from one body part to another, or from one body part to an external or internal force. Pressing is a resistance to gravity, either against a portion of yourself, against space in general or an object. Practice by pressing against yourself, a chair, another person, the wall, table or other objects.

Dabbing and Flicking

Dabbing is sudden, light and direct. It occurs when you dart here and there with pointed gestures of feet and hands, tapping, patting, touching.

Flicking is sudden, light and indirect. It occurs when the hands and feet lead the rest of you, sparking you to action. The fingers become alive, scattering and gathering, and the knees and feet make roundabout gestures in the air, lightly stepping and springing.

Table 4.1 Effort actions

SPACIAL DIRECTION	TIME	WEIGHT	EFFORT ACTION
direct	sudden	strong	punch
direct	sustained	strong	press
direct	sudden	light	dab
direct	sustained	light	glide
indirect	sudden	strong	slash
indirect	sustained	strong	wring
indirect	sudden	light	flick
indirect	sustained	light	float

Actions for flicking and dabbing are small gestures most often with the hands. However, you can flick different substances off various parts of your body or dab different body parts with different substances. For instance, flick a fly off your face, flick water on a piece of paper, dab your fingers in pudding, dab your feet in mud, dab paint on your arm. Coming up with a variety of substances to flick or dab can lead into a scenario in which these become the prime motivation for a relationship.

EXERCISE 4.6 **EXPLORING ACTIONS**

1. Begin in neutral. Start to move in the space in a sustained manner. You speed up and slow down, but you must continue moving in a sustained manner.
2. As you feel the impetus, you can add the styles of actions to your movement. Remain conscious of your breath and emotional state and how it changes as you explore each action.
3. Write down images that evolve from exploring the states.
4. From these images, write two short first-person character sketches/biographies, including place of birth, age, occupation, family background.
5. Also describe the movement qualities of self as character and as part of the gestural language that regulates communication, illustrates a story, indicates emotional state or serves as part of a social communication.

Earth's Elements

Many movement experts believe it is only when we are at one with nature itself that we can fully control, properly tense and fully relax our muscles. Exploring the potential physical life associated with images related to earth elements is one way to manifest Laban's efforts and effort actions. By becoming different elements, you learn to transform from one physical state to another. The explorations operate on two levels of awareness: the discovery of the *subjective* experience of the image as it fuses with your imagination and an *objective* awareness of the experience applied to movement knowledge. You explore the element first as a general abstraction, then as a specific form. For instance, a fire is a general image of an element, while a candle flame, forest fire or camp fire are specific images that can be made even more so by adding adjectives. A candle flame, for example, can be steady, flickering or gentle. The specific images can then become metaphors for the psychological, emotional and physical life of a character.

Beyond expanding the physical imagination, the elements also provide a means to focus on the dramatic principles of stage movement—*phrasing, transitions, intensity, stillness* and *development. Phrasing* is a gesture or series of postures and gestures integral to each other. Consider the two separate actions walking into a room and sitting in a chair. A performance could maintain them as two distinct phrases. However, they could be connected via a *transition*, such as a slight pause prior to sitting down or brushing something off the chair. Brushing the chair could be done with a slashing gesture of the hand or foot that would increase the *intensity* of the transition and thus the intensity of the phrase. Once sitting in the chair, the actor could be absolutely *still* or very restless and could *develop* the moment by working between stillness and activity by using a combination of flicking and dabbing gestures combined with stillness. The initial actions of walking into the room and sitting in a chair have been transformed by use of the dramatic principles of phrasing, transitions, intensity, stillness and development to create a short movement scenario with an implied story line. For each of the earth essence exercises begin and end in neutral.

EXERCISE 4.7 FIRE PHRASING (BEGINNING, MIDDLE AND END)

1. Start to move slowly around the space and focus on the image of fire.
2. Feel the fire move from the center of your pelvis in all directions up through the spine and down through the legs.
3. Feel the fire energy move through you as you begin to be part of the fire—a small, flickering flame that is in constant threat of being put out by water pouring down upon it; an enormous rush of fire as it is pushed forward by an updraft of air; a steady stream of fire that slowly but methodically burns through everything.
4. Be aware of engaging your entire self as a unit, from head through arms, torso, legs and feet. What movement phrases continue to repeat themselves? Be aware that your physical movements have a place of initiation in the body where your breath and the image have fused, spaces of follow through and a point of sending the energy beyond the body. The point of initiation, spaces of follow through and point of sending are the beginning, middle and end of a gesture.
5. Once you have completed the exploration, revisit the experience. Catalogue your memory of the experience through sharing it with others or writing about it in a journal. What parts of your body did you use? What was the phrasing of the energy moving through your body? Which Laban's qualities or effort actions would you use to describe different forms of fire? As you were working, what did you notice about your emotional engagement with different forms of fire?
6. Write down the adjectives or verbs that flow from your unconscious. For example, *fire adjectives* could be *passionate, ardent, fervent, intense* and *irrational*. Also write down *verbs* associated with the action state of fire, such as *ignite, inflame, kindle, light, arouse, excite, insight, inspire, discharge, dismiss, terminate.* The *adjectives* represent possible psychological traits of a character and influence a character's internal monologue. The *verbs* represent the style of a character's physical actions.

EXERCISE 4.8 LIFE CYCLE OF A FIRE (CANDLE FLAME, FOREST FIRE, FIREPLACE FIRE)

Using the same process described for the general fire exercise, explore the life cycle of a specific fire.

1. Begin by picking periods from the life of the fire and then unite them in a series of movements that transform from one movement into the next and have a beginning, middle and end. For instance, the beginning is the initial lighting of the fire,

the middle is the period during which it is burning (and any influences from the environment that might affect its burning) and the end is the fire going out.

2. Some questions to consider are related to phrasing and dramatic intensity: Does the fire start instantly or slowly, burn steadily or erratically? Is it put out quickly, or does it take a period of time for it to go out? Are there moments when the flame is burning with such intensity it is still?

3. Create a name that metaphorically describes your fire piece and perform it for others. Get feedback and revise it to clarify the intentions of the piece as suggested in its name.

EXERCISE 4.9 WATER–TRANSITIONS

1. Begin as in the previous exercise but this time start with a definite form of water. Some possibilities are a flowing river, bubbling brook, ocean waves, drop of water from a faucet, water on an umbrella or edge of a building, an ice cube and steam.

2. Discover the sound associated with the form and incorporate it with the movement.

   Once you feel you have developed one form completely, move onto another until you have a repertoire of movement based on several different forms of water. What Laban qualities are associated with each form of water?

3. Create a nonverbal story that uses phrases from each form of water. What are the possible transitions between one water state and another? Do you find you use sequential or simultaneous movement to transition from one water phrase to another?

4. Repeat the process you used for fire of discovering adjectives and verbs for water. Others have discovered the following *adjectives*: *liquid, graceful, supple, adaptable, adjustable, flexible, accommodating, easygoing* and *changeable*; and the following *verbs*: *alter, transform, vary, adjust, amend, depart, deviate, diverge* and *clash*.

EXERCISE 4.10 WIND–INTENSITY

1. Walk around the room being aware of the breath moving completely through your body, from your feet up through your legs, torso, arms and head.

2. Concentrating both internally and externally, and using the breath as the initiator of the image, allow your body to become a gentle breeze. Are there sounds associated with the breeze?

3. Now feel the breeze picking up intensity as it becomes a rushing wind moving quickly around you and pushing itself through and between your arms and legs. The wind takes on the shape of a small whirlwind as it pushes and brushes across the earth. The whirlwind builds in intensity and then releases back into the rushing wind. Feel the change in intensity of your own breath/energy as it moves with the action of your body.

4. Allow the rushing wind to transform itself into a steady wind that keeps moving and moving, always pushing along the earth. Again feel the change in intensity of your own breath/energy as it moves with the action of your body. What Laban qualities are associated with different forms of wind? *Adjectives for wind* might include *sly, mischievous, playful, indirect*; *verbs* might be *stroke, whip, ruffle, push, fill, propel, surprise, extinguish.*

EXERCISE 4.11 **EARTH–STILLNESS**

1. Make certain that you are released in all your joints from your ankles, knees, hips, spine, shoulders, elbows, wrists and attachment of the head at the top of the spine.
2. Go from walking to a still posture and begin to explore the image of a mountain. Be aware of the highest point on the mountain and its connection to the molten rock that lies below the surface of the Earth.
3. Concentrate on the image, allowing yourself to respond to any mental or physical changes related to it. Where is the center of stillness in your mountain?
4. Start to walk around the room and, as you move, allow the mountain to be transformed into a boulder. Is your boulder moving or still? Rolling? Bouncing? Majestic? Stable?
5. Using your ability to focus on an image, transform the boulder to a small round rock. Where is the physical center of the small round rock? Transform from a small round rock to a grain of sand. Where is the physical center of the grain of sand?
6. If you are working with others, begin to move as a unit as grains of sand blown by the wind. What is your experience of weight and flow as a grain of sand? Other possible earth elements to explore are mud, quicksand, clay, lava (molten and solidified) and an avalanche. What Laban qualities do you associate with different kinds of earth? Possible *earth adjectives*: *solid, earthy, concrete, material, substantial, fixed*; possible *verbs*: *support, defend, bolster, brace, sustain, advance, advocate, champion, promote.*

EXERCISE 4.12 **VEGETATON–DEVELOPMENT**

1. Take time to sit in a park, your back yard, on the beach or other areas with flowers, trees, grass. Incorporate all your senses; focus on a particular tree, bush, flower.
2. Use your eyes to note the shape and varying textures of the plant. Begin to hear the sounds of the plant growing and responding to the wind, earth and animals that live within its environment. Feel the smell of the plant move through your nose and down into your body as you breathe.
3. Depending on where you are, reach out and touch the plant with different parts of your skin. How is the touch of the skin different when you reach with your hands, or your feet, or your arms?

4. Extend your imagination into the cellular structure of the plant as if you were inside it watching it take in carbon dioxide, water and other nutrients as it makes its reach for the sun. See the plant at various stages of its development, from a seed, to seedling, to the beginning development of a bloom or leaves, to full development, to slow decay, and disintegration back into the earth.

5. Returning to the studio, explore the sensory images and experiences from your visit to the park. Try to focus on experiencing movements that are poetic or lyric abstractions of the actual plant and not illustrative or descriptive. Ask what it would feel like to be a tree rather than what does a tree look like?

6. Continue to explore them until you have evolved a movement score that poetically depicts the development of the plant from seedling to mature plant.

Gestures: Social, Functional, Emotional and Motivational

Gestures can be divided into the four categories above, each representing a different function and a broad range of nonverbal language.

Social gestures are culture-specific communications that replace a word with a gesture. These gestures are called *illustrators* and *regulators*. Two examples are the up-and-down gesture of the head to mean "yes" and the two-finger "V for victory" sign. *Illustrators* are used to accent a particular idea and, being context specific, are likely to be understood by two parties in a conversation, despite differences in cultural background. For example, referencing direction or describing how large something is. *Regulators* control the means by which members of a group decide whose turn it is to speak, relying on a variety of facial gestures, eye movements and postural shifts. Regulators are always specific to a community and may also indicate an individual's emotional state.

Functional gestures are daily life physical actions for common tasks such as washing hair, brushing teeth, fixing food and other household tasks. Many household tasks are specific to individual cultural background, occupation and lifestyle. A farmer will incorporate a very different set of gestures than someone who lives in a metropolitan area; a Buddhist will engage very differently in a set of physical actions associated with her faith than a Protestant.

Emotional gestures, or affect displays, are indicators of the mood of the communicator. They include many habitual movements ranging from twisting the hair to tapping the fingers to rearranging elements of clothing. Cultural norms often dictate the degree and form of emotional display appropriate for given situations.

Motivational gestures have the specific goal of influencing the behavior of others. We think of them in terms of either their momentary or their long-term function. Emotional and motivational gestures can overlap in the moment with social and functional gestures. For example, politicians shake people's hands at rallies as a social gesture (greeting), but attempt to convey an attitude in doing so that motivates the individual to vote for them.

EXERCISE 4.13 ELEMENTS/ESSENCE/CHARACTER

While exploring the elements, you have evolved adjectives and playable verbs for each element.

1. Using adjectives and verbs from the different elements, explore the forms of gestures—social, functional, emotional and motivational. For example, gestures derived from work with the fire element. What is a passionate shake of the hand? What is it to intensely get a drink of water? What is an ardent response to good news? What is a fervent appeal to a group of people? Try more than one solution for any of the gesture categories. From what emotional centers do these gestures emerge?
2. Using one of the earth's elements as the basis for a character's personality, answer the following: Who are they? What is important to them in the world? What do they want from life? What is their internal monologue? Use the physical vocabulary of the earth element to explore the movement and gestural language of the character. How does the character walk, stand and wait, sit, pick up a telephone, run to meet someone, open a door to a friend, feed a pet, present themselves at a cocktail party or interact with others?
3. Once you have fully developed this character, write a description of the character. Repeat the process with other earth elements. Ultimately, you should have five different character studies, one for each earth element.

Observation and Analysis

As a performer, you are always observing the world for images to file away in your memory to retrieve when necessary to create a character. The majority of these observations are informal responses to people you see walking on the street, in a restaurant or visiting a museum. Periodically, you are cast in a role that requires a formal method of observation. The approach provided in this chapter combines your understanding of Laban efforts and effort actions with your ability to observe the movement choices of another.

Observing the movement of others is a process that incorporates many of the skills you have already learned, including relaxation, concentration, focus and awareness. Some of your best behavior observations take place in malls or outdoor cafes that allow you to find a comfortable place to sit and watch the life around you. Moreover, media provide the opportunity to gain a vast array of information from "surfing" evangelical church services, cooking shows, home videos, MTV, Country-Western music stations, in addition to art exhibitions and exhibits.

Wherever your observation takes place, the following set of guidelines will help you observe effectively. Make certain that you have a comfortable place from which to observe and place yourself in a relatively inconspicuous position in relation to those you are observing. Allow yourself to focus in a relaxed manner on your subject, initially answering general questions concerning the general posture and changes in posture of the individual. Jot down notes on the time and place of observation, who was observed (young woman, old man, etc.) and a general description of their movement. After a period of general observations begin to look for the following: (1) the shape of the hand so that it shows clearly how an object is held, (2) the rhythm that evolves from a repeated action, (3) the weight, time and space qualities of any movement or gesture, (4) the quality of transition between movements or gestures, (5) how much of the body is involved in a physical movement or gesture, (6) the rhythm of the body's movements, (7) the mood associated with movement or gesture and (8) vocal patterns associated with the gestural pattern.

After a period of observing, take yourself out of the observing mode and into recuperation. This recuperative moment can be as short as looking away for a brief moment, or as thoughtful as getting up and relocating yourself in another position from which to observe. The more you apply the technique of relaxed focus, the easier it will be to maintain your concentration. An accurate analysis is the accumulation of several phases of observation. As you complete each, ask yourself, using the chart provided below, "What yet do I not know?" You want to create a "thick description" of the person. These observations can be compared with the self-observation of Chapter 1 and serve as the beginning of a character notebook that you can expand upon and use whenever you need help in creating a new character.

This method of observation can also be used to develop a character from visual sources, applying the same analytical process to drawings and paintings of people from a particular historical period, or to photographs of people taken from written and filmed ethnographies, magazines or collections of photographs. Building this form of research into your working life as an actor, you will develop during your career a notebook of invaluable resource material.

EXERCISE 4.14 OUTLINE FOR ANALYSIS

The following outline includes information you will want to record for anyone you are observing. Ultimately, you will develop a detailed account of the movement of the person you are observing. You may discover you like to draw sketches to accompany written observations or supplement the written document with photos or videotaped material. The goal is to organize a set of data that you can refer to as needed in the development of characters.

1. **Where Observed:** Did the observation take place in a shopping mall, restaurant, street corner, theatre, dance club, museum, home, video store, etc?
2. **Who Observed:** Whom did you observe—an individual, a group? If possible include a short biographical statement, including information on age, gender, ethnic identity, place of birth, education, etc.
3. **Context of Observation:** Describe location and interactions that took place as part of it. For instance, if you were observing children in a park, did you talk to them? What was the nature of the conversation? Or was your observation based on secondary source material, such as a video, historical account, television, film?
4. **Most Active Body Parts:** What are the most active body parts of the person

observed—legs, arms, torso, head, hands, feet? What are they doing—sitting, standing, moving?

5. **Use of Space:** When the person moves through space, what direction does he/she take with their body? Is the path direct or indirect? The specific direction of movement? Or moving in general? Do they carry themselves away from gravity or are they released into gravity? When moving, how much space do they cover? What is the size and shape of the bubble that surrounds them? What about when they are sitting?

6. **Organization of Body Parts Within Phrased Movement (Gestures):** Does the gesture language tend to be simultaneous, sequential, or in some combination of the two?

7. **Forms of Gesture, or Kinesthetic Display:** What forms of gesture is the person most likely to engage—social, illustrators, regulators, functional, emotional, motivational? Can you supplement the written document with photos or videotaped material?

8. **Use of Effort:** What is the person's general affinity toward flow, weight, time and space? Can their movement be summed up as falling into either the resistant or the indulgent categories? What body parts initiate changes in posture or gesture?

9. **Combinations and Transitions:** What effort actions tend to be combined? What action qualities? Is there a way the person under observation organizes the muscle system to make transitions between gestures with differing qualities?

10. **Interactions:** How do they use their eyes or other body parts in interactions with others? Direct? Indirect? Combination? Do their movements, including touching others, have a tendency to be sustained, sudden, combination? An individual? A group? A person from the opposite or same sex? Are they fluid, bound or a combination of both in their interactions with others?

11. **Metaphors:** What metaphors would you use to describe this person? Write down the adjectives or verbs that flow from your unconscious. For example, *fire adjectives* could be *passionate, ardent, fervent, intense, irrational.* Also include *verbs* associated with the action state of fire.

Summary

This chapter has provided you with an opportunity to expand your energy system and your kinesthetic awareness through a focus on Laban's efforts and effort action categories. The use of images throughout has expanded your physical imagination and the possible gestural language of a character. It has also provided an opportunity to use earth elements to increase your awareness of dramatic principles of stage movement—*phrasing, transitions, intensity, stillness* and *development.* Finally, Laban's approach has provided you with a method of observation and analysis that you can use as part of the research for character studies.

CHAPTER 5 CHARACTER CREATION

Character Creation

Exploring physical action in the development of a character

> *By doing character analysis and research, you feel secure in what you are playing. The audience may not see what you did, but they see the confidence and security.*
>
> **Benicio Del Toro, actor**

Creating a character brings together all aspects of your acting and movement training. It is a three-stage process which includes a period of investigation in which you research the facts of the play's context, a period of inference in which you begin to surmise the details of your character, and a period of invention and embodiment where you use your imagination to create the physical life of the character. The exercises in this chapter begin with investigation of the character's social/cultural history. This is followed by exercises that consider the similarities and differences between you and the character, and an exercise to activate your imagination to provide more detail for creating the character. The archetype exercise provides an opportunity to explore various characters that are consistently a part of our narratives in books, film and television. Finally, there are points of exploration for developing the embodiment of a character.

> *The more often I re-live the physical life the more definite and firm will the line of the spiritual life become. The more often I feel the merging of these two lines, the more strongly will I believe in the psycho-physical truth of this state and the more firmly will I feel the two levels of my part. The physical being of a part is good ground for the seed of the spiritual being to grow.*
>
> **Constantin Stanislavski**

Investigation

Each script and production represents a complex system of disparate viewpoints united and brought to life on stage through dramatic imagination. It is often referred to as the world of the play, within which groups interact with belief systems, social structures, aesthetic ideals and communication modes. A character's actions are related to a specific community's world view which is influenced by geography and the way in which environment is internalized as religious beliefs (such as whether spiritual power is centered in the cathedral or the forest, etc.). All these influence the development of social groups, forms of government, family dynamics and daily individual physical tasks.

A script's world of the play can be researched by examining associated art forms, including paintings, dance, music, literature and architecture, that provide information on possible general clothing styles, body stances and movement vocabulary. Information can also be gathered from travel books, social manners guides, biographical material, journals, collected letters and historical accounts which define rituals taking place at fixed times within societal cycles based on seasons, climate, historical events and life cycle celebrations. From the above sources, you can discover greetings, physical stances, gestural communication styles and the use of spatial distance. This section includes a list of detailed questions that you can use to create a description of the world of the play, its cultural parameters and its movement vocabulary.

EXERCISE 5.1 **WORLD OF THE PLAY**

You can enter a new world if you can understand about the sense of time, space, place, values, structure, beauty, sex, recreation, and how these are manifested through sight and sound for those who live there. These questions apply to information in the script and to research on the world of the play.

1. **TIME**—How **rapidly** does it move for most people? How **conscious** are they of time passing? How do they **record** or note time? What is the dominant **tempo/ rhythm**? Do people **focus** mainly on the moment, on whole lifetimes, the future, the past? In what **point in history** is the play set, written, performed? How do these interact? How far does the audience or play **move** out of its own time?
2. **SPACE**—How is it **defined** and viewed? Is it literal, spiritual, philosophical or abstract? How large a **bubble** do people carry around? How do **personal** spaces alter? How flexible? To what degree is **privacy** respected? What are attitudes toward **invasion** and force? How is space **violated**? How do these beliefs **translate** into audience proximity and movement patterns?
3. **PLACE**—Is the **setting** rural, metro, coastal, inland, protected, exposed, confined, open? **Age**? Is it new or old? What **influence** do terrain, flora, fauna and weather have? Does the place have a specific or generic **character**? How aware are people of **other** places? How **provincial** is their perspective? Are they **citizens** only of this spot or of the world? What is the **relationship to nature**? To what extent is the environment altered or accepted?
4. **VALUES**—What are the **beliefs** most widely **shared**? What ideals? What are the **traditions** and how large is the commitment to them? How are **friendship, family, trust** and **community** defined and how are these **bonds broken?** What is the

predominant **mood**? Who are role models, heroes, **idols**? What are shared **fantasies** and ideal futures? How do they define **sin**, consequences, forgiveness, ethics, justice? What gets **attention**? What holds it? Value placed on **money**? Uses for it? What is the place of **God** and the church in life? What kind of **humor** dominates? What role has laughter in society? How is **fear** defined? What are its sources and how do people cope with it? How and to what degree is **emotion** expressed? How suppressed?

5. **STRUCTURE—Who leads** and who follows? How easy is it to bring about **change or justice**? How absolute is **authority**? What is the voice of the individual? What is the government **system**? How is **daily life** ordered? How is **family** defined? How are **etiquette** and rules set? How much emphasis is on **education**? How are **groups** created and identified? Which are most powerful? What **professions** dominate and how is **work** viewed? How is **information** gathered and spread?

6. **BEAUTY—What is the look most aspired to** in this group? Who are the contemporary **ideals** of perfection? What part does **fitness** play in physical attractiveness? What is the relationship between beauty, health and **comfort**? Which **colors**, **textures**, **silhouettes** are favored? How important is **fashion**? How fast does it **change**? To what degree is **nature** altered in order to create a thing of beauty? How is **taste** defined? What are favored modes of **artistic expression**?

7. **SEX—**How significant to the collective **consciousness** is sex? What are considered **turn-ons** and **turn-offs**? Which **areas of anatomy** are revealed, concealed, emphasized? What are sexual **stereotypes**? How is **sexuality communicated**? How is **seduction** defined? Is the **emphasis** on the act or the chase? On pleasure or procreation? What is the standard **courtship ritual**? How much tolerance for **deviation**? What are the accepted attitudes toward **infidelity**, toward **promiscuity**? What **degree of suppression or expression** of sexuality occurs?

8. **RECREATION—**What is most people's idea of **fun**? What would be an **ideal social occasion**? An enjoyable day? What is the **participation** level? Are they doers or watchers? **Intellectual** life? Thinkers or mindless hedonists? What are common shared hobbies and **pastimes**? What are differences between **sexes**? **Consumption**? Favored and coveted meals, drink, drugs? What is the relative **importance** of recreation in life? The standard view of **indulgence**?

9. **SIGHT—**How do all the above manifest themselves in the way the world looks, in **shapes, angles, light, shadow, patterns of movement**? In **clothing**, furnishings, props, hairdos and jewelry? What is the pattern of **movement** and **contact** and its significance?

10. **SOUND—**How does it come out in **speech** and **nonverbal** communication? To what degree are **listening** and **speaking** prized? What **vocal quality** is most desired, rewarded, emulated and for what reasons? Is there **standardized** pronunciation or great variance? Which part of pitch register is employed? Is the **word choice** vague or direct? What is the role of **music** and **dance** in life?

SHORT SUMMARY

Use this condensed version of the checklist to help review the basic concepts and in your investigation:

1. Time—Tempo/rhythm? Age? Point in history?
2. Space—Bubbles? Privacy? Invasion?
3. Place—Setting? Relationship to nature? Awareness of others?
4. Values—Mood? Ideals? Money? God? Emotion?
5. Structure—Government? Daily life? Education?
6. Beauty—Looks? Comfort? Artistic expression?
7. Sex—Expression? Seduction? Courtship?
8. Recreation—Occasions? Participation? Consumption?
9. Sight—Stillness? Movement? Ritual?
10. Sound—Language? Listening? Music?

Dramaturge Help

More and more productions engage a dramaturge who is in charge of historical and literary research. This staff member has been working on the script for a long time prior to casting and first rehearsals, consulting with the director and other staff as the production concept and designs have evolved. A good dramaturge will have meticulously researched many of the very

"I enjoy role-playing, but do we really need the dramaturge?"

Figure 5.1 Dramaturge. Copyright Tort.

issues raised in the world of the play analysis. Usually the dramaturge has strongly developed research skills and has found numerous sources that most of us have not even considered, with extensive information regarding placing the play in its historical context and tracing the history and impact of past productions. Make use of the expertise and depth of knowledge the dramaturge can offer as this can help you save time and move forward more rapidly in your own knowledge of the universe in which your character exists. Along with numerous other duties, the dramaturge often observes rehearsals and offers notes to help you remain true to the play and the character.

Inference and Invention

Once you have completed the first stage in creating the world of the character, investigating the play's world, the second step is to read and examine the script, noting the character's specific given circumstances: the who, what, when and where of age, occupation, family background. Next, review and note all the phrases and words that pertain to the character in the script—either said by him/her or by someone else. These phrases will provide metaphors for movement explorations. From this, write a character biography. The act of writing helps to solidify the information in your imagination. Include in this biography answers to the following questions:

EXERCISE 5.2 **CHARACTER BIOGRAPHY**

1. Where was the character born?
2. Who were his/her parents?
3. Where did he/she go to elementary, secondary school or higher education?
4. Who were the significant people in his/her life as a child?
5. As an adult?
6. How does the character describe him/herself physically, including clothing styles?
7. What is his/her occupation?
8. What religious system does the character believe in?
9. How does the character feel about the current circumstances of his/her life?
10. Who would the character turn to in time of trouble?
11. Who would the character help if they were in trouble?
12. I describe others as . . .
13. In groups, I tend to . . .
14. My favorite things are . . .
15. I am most and least interested in . . .
16. My goals are to . . .
17. Primary obstacle to achieving this goal is . . .
18. My usual strategy and tactics for success are . . .
19. My best possible future would be . . . My worst possible future would be . . . My wildest dreams come true would be . . .

Your investigation also needs to consider you, the actor, as a person with a particular personal history and life experience in order to understand the potential physical challenges this character creates for you as an actor. How do you get from you to him/her? You may be playing a character that is physically aggressive with others. In contrast, you are, as an individual, passive rather than aggressive in your physical interactions. Or the character you are playing may demand you learn a specific skill, to know how to juggle, do a somersault, dance a jig, etc.

EXERCISE 5.3 SELF TO CHARACTER

Explore how your life is similar to or distinct from the character by asking yourself the same questions you asked for the character. From this, write a short self-description and answer the following questions.

1. My physical life varies from the actor playing me in the following ways. For example, you can use the Laban efforts to make a distinction between yourself and the character. Such as, I have a tendency to move strongly and directly and the character is lighter in touch and more indirect in the use of physical tactics.
2. The actor playing me needs to use the Magic If or answer the question: What would I do if I were in the circumstances of this character?

The combination of information about self and character is the basis for the invention of the character's physical life. Answer the following with as much detail as possible. You may find that your answers change throughout the rehearsal period.

EXERCISE 5.4 CHARACTER'S BODY RECIPE

1. **Standing and Sitting:** ~~How old are you~~

    How old are you?
    What gender?
    Have you experienced this before?

    What is your character's width of stance?

    Is it ruled by gravity and strong or air and is light?

    Are your character's feet turned in, out or forward?

    Where is your character's weight held? In pelvis, chest, head?

    What is your character's relationship of head to chest?

    Relationship of arms to legs?

    What are some of your character's conventional hand positions?

    What is the outline of your character's silhouette? Standing? Sitting? Lying?

    How do they sit? stand?

2. **Expression:**

In your interactions with others are you direct or indirect, quick or slow to respond?

What is your character's primary emotional center?

What physical attributes of another attracts your character?

How does your character indicate physical interest in another?

How does your character respond to touching? And with whom?

How does your character initiate touching? And with whom?

How does your character act upon urgency?

How does your character engage in positions of power or dominance?

How does your character react to situations of fear, loss of control, terror?

How does your character physically protect themself?

3. **Tempo/Rhythm and Motion:**   *— Move on a grid*

What is the general tempo/rhythm of your character?

Does your character move with fluid ease through situations or is there a sense of bound control?

Is this different for different situations?

What is the size of your character's space bubble?

How does your character's space bubble change in different social situations?

What is the physical expression of your character's status in the world?

4. **Gestures and Adaptations:**

What gestural style is most common to your character?

Is your character indulgent with gestures that are light, free, indirect and quick, or is your character more restrained with gestures that are strong, bound, direct and sustained?

How does your character adapt his/her general gestural tendency in new situations?

What situations call for the most extensive adaptations?

5. **Cultural Binding and Mannerisms:**

What cultural influences go into creating your character's social presentation? How does this influence your character's social interactions?

> Are there different social masks for different situations?
>
> What mannerisms does your character have? Are they the result of cultural surroundings or idiosyncratic to them?
>
> 6. **Metaphor:**
>
> What earth element would your character be? (Following completion of the section on archetype, what archetype would the character be?)

Activating the Imagination

The imagination, according to Stanislavski, is a pivotal component of the actor's craft. "An actor's imagination can draw to itself the life of another person, adapt it, and discover mutual and exciting qualities and features." Your artistic imagination unites your life, experience and creativity with the inner world of dreams, a world in which:

> *We can use our inner eye to see all sorts of visual images, living creatures, human faces, their features, landscapes, and the material world of objects, settings, and so forth. With our inner ear we can hear all sorts of melodies, voices, intonations, and so forth. We can feel things in the imagination at the prompting of our sensation and emotion memory.*

Stanislavski divided the imagination into two types, *passive* and *active*. In *passive imagination*, you are an observer of the details of a setting but do not necessarily interact with it, literally setting the stage in your imagination. In a state of *active imagination*, you actively engage in playing a role within the imagined environment. Both forms of imagination necessitate focusing on a set of sensory images. This requires the ability to concentrate on a set of images for an extended period of time as one might when day dreaming.

To activate your imagination, you engage in a dialogue with images from a state of relaxed readiness that is a version of the "Here and Now" exercises from Chapter 1 (see pages 16 and 23). The breath is focused, the muscles are released but ready to move and you are attending to your environment with all your senses. Participation in the imagined event moves the experience from the realm of pure fantasy to *active imagination*, the space in which your conscious and unconscious minds meet in a purely symbolic experience of images. The process is in three steps: inviting the unconscious, dialoging the experience and creating a performance based on the experience.

EXERCISE 5.5 IMAGINATION ACTIVATION

1. Invite the unconscious. Provide yourself with a quiet working space in which you can lie or sit and focus on your breath. Maintain this focus until you feel a state of internal quiet. From this state, begin to place yourself in a specific environment, a city park, the redwoods, an ocean beach or other location.
2. Note the environment in detail, including the color and shape of different parts of it, the smells, quality of light, the sounds associated with it. Notice a path or method, such as a specific mode of transportation, that allows you to navigate through this environment. While traveling on this path, note the changes in the path as you observe it from different positions.
3. You are stopped by someone or something that represents a challenge. Fulfill the requirements of the challenge and continue on the path. Before you complete your journey, you will be stopped two other times. In each case, fulfill the requirements of the challenge. On completing the final challenge, allow yourself to find your final destination.
4. Write down a detailed description of your experience. From this create a series of actions that represents the story.
5. Use the score to create a short movement sketch that tells the story of your journey.

Archetype

> *Myth is the secret opening through which the inexhaustible energies of the cosmos pour into human cultural manifestations. It has always been the prime function of mythology and rite to supply the symbols that move the human spirit forward.*
>
> **Joseph Campbell, mythologist**

Investigation, inference and invention can often be summed up in a metaphor that is the revelation of an archetype, a recurrent personality that exists in all narratives. From early writings of Plato through Jung, whose are most often referenced, to current pop culture references, the use of the archetype as a point of reference is constant. The term originates from the ancient Greek "archos" (original or old) and "typos" (pattern, model or type). The archetypes may be organized with as few as eight or as many as twenty, breaking down characteristics into more specific types. Not to be confused with stereotypes or the tendency to exhibit clichéd behavior, archetypes are far more profound and fundamental human motifs, evoking deep emotions. Joseph Campbell, in a series of books that includes *Hero of a Thousand Faces*, has illustrated the symbolic similarity of archetypes among the myths of various cultural groups. According to Campbell, a primary function of performance is to dramatize these archetypal forces. Edward Whitmont, a proponent of Campbell's ideas, writes:

> *The profoundly moving cathartic effect which dramatic art continues to exert through all the ages may well be based upon its presenting us with a mirror of soul and life in the theme of men and women against their destinies.*

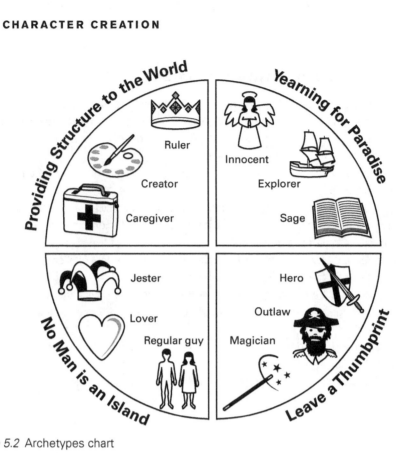

Figure 5.2 Archetypes chart

You as a performer are the means by which these values and ideals achieve embodiment. What follows are twelve archetypes divided into four areas of desire: 1) to be yourself, 2) having an impact through leaving a thumbprint, 3) creating stability and structure and 4) belonging to a group. Each represents an overall aspect of a character's personality. The archetype also blends positive and negative traits, either of which in any situation can influence a character's behavior. While you may prefer to ignore the shadow or negative side, knowledge of it helps you appreciate a character's internal obstacles.

The Twelve Archetypes

BEING YOURSELF

1. Innocent (Impulse to find out about the world—Yearning for paradise, learning and identity)

Children are innocents who have completely accepted the values of the group to which they are born, which does not mean they are always in a caring environment, only that they accepted the world as experienced without question. This archetype represents people who wear and believe without question the social masks of the group to which they were born. The desire of the innocent is to remain in safety, while the greatest fear is abandonment.

Potential associated images: Newborns of any kind.

Shadow side: An unwillingness to accept change in the world, as new experience represents dissolution of the order of the mask, which may cause them unwittingly to hurt themselves by setting limits to self-growth and inner knowing, as the innocent refuses to acknowledge difference.

Potential shadow images: Objects that are difficult to move such as a large boulder.

2. **Seeker/Explorer (Freedom to experience—Don't fence me in—Seeking a better, more fulfilling life)**

Seekers are way-showers and wanderers who search life's pathways. They have a constant desire for enlightened transformation and to brave the unknown, strongly believing in the perfectibility of existence and always searching for a better way of life. A seeker's greatest fear is becoming trapped in the culturally normative.

Potential images: Natural spaces representing journeys or emotional retreat such as deserts, woods, oceans, outer space.

Shadow side: This is the restless perfectionist for whom nothing is ever quite enough.

Potential shadow image: A person who is obsessive about neatness, organization, dress, etc.

3. **Sage (To discover the truth, which will set you free—Using intelligence and analysis to understand the world)**

This is the spiritual teacher who is gifted in inspiring others and helping them to make ideas tangible. A teacher, the sage is a sleuth who asks questions about the nature of existence and then guides students to answers, wishing to promote truth and understanding. Fear for the sage rests with the potential of failing to find the path to wisdom.

Potential images: Elders, animals, places or things.

Shadow side: A heartless rational judge of knowledge or people.

Potential shadow image: Frozen in an unyielding attitude.

HAVING AN IMPACT

4. **Warrior/Champion (Proving one's worth through courage—Desire to leave a special lasting thumbprint on the world)**

This archetype maintains strong boundaries while pursuing a desire to serve the community as protector. Warriors want to win and succeed, usually by overcoming a set of obstacles. The warrior's greatest fear is displaying any appearance of weakness or loss of power.

Potential images: Armor, walls, animals of size.

Shadow side: A villain who uses the ability to mentally and emotionally dominate others for personal gain.

Potential shadow side images: An asymmetrical face and body such as Shakespeare's Richard III.

5. **Destroyer/Outlaw/Rebel (To destroy/overturn what is not working—Revenge or revolution—Rules are made to be broken)**

Destroyers transform themselves and their environment, doing away with one situation and replacing it with another. This personality is closely allied with death and rebirth. Fulfillment is found in growth and metamorphosis due to boredom in a routine life that feels like stagnation.

Potential images: Natural disasters—forest fires, typhoons, whirlwinds, tidal waves.

Shadow side: The addictive side of this personality can lead to self-destruction through undermining relationships, careers, etc.

Potential shadow images: Drug addicts, crisis oriented people, Jobba the Hut from Star Wars.

6. **Magician (Making things happen—Transforming the world to their vision—Making dreams come true)**

This archetype has an artful sense of flexibility in all aspects of communication and the ability to transform a moment from negative to positive with the intent of moving reality from lesser to better states. Magicians fear that their personal power will not be enough to overcome any evil.

Potential images: Constant transformation from one energy construct to another, movement from animal to people, people to inanimate objects, morphing.

Shadow side: The opposite of working for benefit by using tricks to diminish what might be possible.

Potential shadow images: Power used to control and limit others.

CREATING STABILITY

7. **Caregiver (Protecting others—Providing structure to the world—Desire to feel safe and in control)**

This is a parent figure that has a love of nature and of beauty, receptive, with a nurturing balance of emotions. The chief desire of the caregiver is to make a difference through helping others. The biggest fear is becoming ruled by their selfishness.

Potential images: Caves, coves and hidden places that provide refuge, a tree of life.

Shadow side: The suffering martyr, whose means of controlling others involves manipulating the feelings through guilt.

Potential shadow images: A continually nagging sound in the background—a faucet with a constant drip.

8. **Creator (Causing enduring value—If it can be imagined it can be done—Realizing a vision)**

This is someone always focusing on the awakening of new life, needing to be involved in conceiving something new—a piece of art, a new company, a new invention or a new life. The creator's greatest fear is lack of imagination.

Potential image: The promise present in the birth of a child.

Shadow side: Creation run amuck, destroying in the act of creation, developing too much of anything—people, technology, food, etc.

Potential shadow image: Overly rapid technological change, a new processing program every week, change that is not needed.

9. **Ruler (Leadership and control—Power is what is most important—Desire to create stable community)**

A ruler feels responsible for creating a life or a government that is harmonious and prosperous, a mediator, adjuster or arbitrator who has a deep love of simplicity, fairness and balance. A ruler fears those forces within self, nature or the group that create chaos.

Potential image: A person standing in perfect symmetry.

Shadow side: This is the unreasonable dictator indulging whims at the expense of others.

Potential shadow image: Any dictator who oppresses others.

BELONGING

10. **Orphan/Every person (Connecting to and fitting in with others—Desiring group membership—No person is an island—Desire to belong and feel valued)**

People that respond to various social groups but do not know to which they belong, so they are in a state of conflict. While they desire to be part of a group, they fear they will be exploited or victimized by any to which they are a part.

Potential images: An isolated plant, animal, rock or person.

Shadow side: A tendency to play the perpetual victim, with a consequent lack of self responsibility and a tendency to blame others for the circumstances of life.

Potential shadow images: A hermit, a homeless person.

11. **Lover (Experiencing bliss—Desire to be in a relationship of intimacy, surrounded by love)**

The aspiration of the lover is the bliss to be found in unity with another. This archetype expresses a multifaceted passion for all of life's experiences, embodying gifts of perception, extended vision, insight and intuition caused by the marriage of the masculine and feminine within the self. The greatest fear is loss of love and disconnection from the other.

Potential images: Flowers in various stages—buds, unfolding, full bloom.

Shadow side: The use of sexuality to gain emotional control over others for either short- or long-term personal fulfillment.

Potential shadow image: Hidden thorns on a rose bush.

12. **Fool/Jester (To live in the moment because you only live once—Desire to have a great time and lighten up the world)**

This personality is filled with mirth, humor and sexual appetite, taking many forms, the wise fools and buffoons of Shakespeare, the outrageous and clumsy fools of farce, and the modern fools of the theatre of the absurd. The fool is our inner child that knows how to play, to be sensual and in the body, filled with vitality and aliveness, expressing primitive, childlike, spontaneous, playful creativity. The joy of the fool is in pleasure and aliveness; the fear is that pleasure will be taken away.

Potential images: People's actions that make us smile, laugh, guffaw, snicker, chuckle, grin, smirk, leer, sneer. Charlie Chaplin. Kristen Wiig. Bill Irwin.

Shadow side: The clown can turn frantic and become entirely defined by lusts and other urges without any self-control.

Potential shadow image: A glass of wine that constantly replenishes itself and causes the fool to loose control.

EXERCISE 5.6 ARCHETYPAL INVENTORY

This exercise helps you to better understand the myths and related archetypes that influence your character's life. Answer the following questions as your character:

1. What are the primary stories from your character's childhood? They can be fairy tales or stories that were read to your character. Once you have identified the story or stories, describe the personality of the primary characters.
2. During your character's life, have there been real or fictional characters who were heroes for you? Potential examples could come from television or film, novels or politics. Describe the hero.
3. What is your character's family history? Are there special people or stories that seem central to the family's view of themselves in the world?
4. What is your character's explanation for how the world functions? Do you believe in the Bible, the Koran, Torah, karma, a pantheon of gods or alien beings? Do you have any daily or seasonal rituals associated with this set of beliefs?
5. Watch television for several hours, channel surfing if possible. What stories and people would your character most identify with?
6. Identify an archetype for your character. What are the potential images associated with it, both positive and shadow?

EXERCISE 5.7 **EXPLORING AN ARCHETYPE**

This exercise is one way to discover the psychological and physical life of both sides of each archetype. It requires that you maintain a state of relaxed concentration to allow the energy of the image to flow through your body.

1. Choose an archetype to work with, move to some part of the room and assume a position, either lying, sitting or standing. With your internal eye, review the archetype you want to investigate. What are its primary attributes? What are some potential images associated with the archetype?
2. Once you have taken time to analyze the archetype in reference to your character and determine an appropriate image, bring yourself to neutral. With each inward breath imagine the image inhabiting every cell of your body, from the soles of your feet to the palms of your hands and the top of your head. Your entire self becomes a conduit for the archetypal image.
3. Filled with the energy of the image, start to move around the room as the archetype. An internal monologue may instantly begin to form—do not be afraid to express it verbally. In fact, the physical personality of the archetype becomes a more rooted and powerful experience if you verbally express these thoughts. From the mind of the archetype, answer the following questions: What is my primary motivation in the world? What is it I need most from other people? What gives me the greatest joy? The greatest pain? What is my most treasured memory?
4. Once you feel you have thoroughly explored the archetype, stop, gently shake out all parts of your body and return to dynamic neutral. Give yourself the opportunity to explore all the archetypes from their positive aspects.
5. Repeat the exploration with an image from the shadow side of the archetype. During the working session you will discover that the image evolves and changes. Do not try to prevent it. It is only necessary to stay kinesthetically connected to the energy of the image through the use of the breath.

Archetypes Everywhere

While those explored above are the most common, archetypes appear in numerous shapes, sizes and variations. Offstage, it can be helpful to know which archetypes are at play in oneself and others, especially loved ones, friends and co-workers, in order to gain personal insight into behaviors and motivations.

Investigate as many as possible and recognize them in whatever form they appear as there are many useful ones to assist in developing characterization. Our most popular and indelible stories invariably work variations on classic archetypes.

Points of Exploration

You have evolved an expanded awareness of your personal movement tendencies, discovered the functioning of the bony, muscle and joint systems, explored the effort qualities, learned to use imagery in the creation of a physical character, developed your observational skills, learned how to investigate a script to create the world of the play, experienced the potential of the imagination and explored the perspective of archetypes. Points of exploration provide an opportunity to focus on one area from this new knowledge base and ultimately expand that to incorporate the whole life of the character. Any aspect from the exercises you have learned can be a point of exploration. The exercises in this section concentrate on two fundamental skills in the evolution of a character: the use of breath in the embodiment of an image and the ability to explore a space. Thus, they provide a model that can be used for other explorations.

EXERCISE 5.8 BREATH AND IMAGE EXPLORATION

Breath, as a point of exploration, can be combined with imagery obtained from working with Laban's efforts and metaphors. This can be an animal, an earth essence derived from the natural mask work or an archetype.

1. Once you have picked a metaphor, see it approximately two feet in front of you either standing or floating in space.
2. Activating your imagination, watch the metaphor, if nonhuman, become human by developing an upright position with spine, legs, feet, arms, hands and head. Add details to the image such as color of hair, position of head, spine, legs and arms. Once you have flushed out all the aspects of the image, take a breath in and as you breathe out step into the image.
3. Continuing to focus on the breath and the related image, feel the image move through your body's structure. Feel the image transforming your body on a cellular level, realigning your pelvis, spine, arms, hands and face as well as legs and feet.
4. Once you have aligned yourself with the image, begin to explore different gestures, postures and forms of movement. See the environment around you with the character's eyes, hear with his/her ears, smell with their nose, touch with their skin.
5. In the rehearsal process, you may discover that there is really more than one image that is important to your understanding of the character. For example, the actor playing Jim in the "Gentleman Caller" scene from Tennessee Williams' *Glass Menagerie* could approach the scene as if he were a steady wind and the actor playing Laura as if she were a delicate flower. Or, they could approach the scene with Jim as a giant bear and Laura as a lap dog. Or, they could approach the scene with Jim as a warrior and Laura as an orphan.

An element of nonverbal communication is the space with which we surround ourselves (as in the bubble discussed earlier) and the related aspect of touch. In acting terms, this space is the "where" of a character's life that can be divided into personal and public space. Our experience of personal space is situational and culturally specific.

Anthropologist Edward Hall has documented the spatial or bubble preferences for different cultural groups, dividing space into intimate, personal, social and public. His research suggests that northern Europeans prefer a large spatial distance between themselves and others, while people from the Mediterranean area are comfortable with closer physical contact. Space and the degree of touch, appropriate or inappropriate, is related to social station, gender status and cultural upbringing.

There are also distinctive spatial relationships between genders—males/males, females/females and females/males. According to performance theorist Richard Schechner, space is alive with potential in the interaction of individual sensory systems and the environment. It is a communication from within the spaces of the body to the spaces within the environment.

EXERCISE 5.9 SPACE EXPLORATION

1. While in the process of exploring space, consider the activity in terms of words with associative meaning such as investigate, search and venture. Note how much you can observe about the space by first focusing on the use of your eyes, followed by closing your eyes and concentrating on what you hear, then what you smell and finally what you feel. Each of these sensory states particularizes the initial state of exploration.
2. Next you can begin to consider how your character moves through space. For example, you can use Laban's effort actions to consider whether he/she moves directly, attempting to penetrate, invade or puncture people, furniture or the space itself as he/she moves through it. Or is his/her attitude toward space constantly shifting in a series of indirect choices?
3. When the character enters a room or sits in a chair, does he/she *fill* the room with his/her presence or take over a chair? Characters who fill the space are attempting to project themselves into an entire area. Methods of filling an area include *spreading, sprawling, draping, permeating* and *expanding*. What is the statement you make about your personal boundary by how you fill the space?
4. Characters can also *surround* objects and people or *repulse* them. In surrounding something or someone, you are literally attempting to *encircle, envelop, enclose* or *embrace* them or it with your arms, legs, trunk and head. Characters can also move through settings by *crossing* them—*ford, span, traverse*—in space, *advancing* through them—*promote, progress, exalt*—in space, or *retreating—escape, withdraw, retire*—from them.

Each of these approaches to space can influence the action/objective score you have created. Which seem like choices the character might make? Which are completely outside the realm of your character? Which might be something they might do under certain circumstances? What are those circumstances?

Summary

This chapter has provided you with a method to integrate your movement knowledge and acting background to create a character, including investigation and researching the context of the world of the play, inference in discovering the physical life of the character from the perspective of your body recipe and imagination through activating your physical imagination. You also have had an opportunity to explore your character's relationship to culturally prevalent archetypes. The points of exploration have provided a road map for using the approaches of Laban, archetypes or social/cultural attitudes as the focus for further investigation, invention and imagination.

CHAPTER 6 ACTING SPACES

Acting Spaces

Negotiating stage spaces for movement mastery

> *The place where you stand, the way you use your space, how you are in relation to other people in scenes, how you dance with them, that's what acting's all about.*
>
> **Sean Connery, actor**

Movement Maneuvers

The Acting Space

So far we have focused just on you and your instrument. We now consider the stage space you inhabit. Theatre can take place anywhere from street corners to warehouses, but the proscenium style auditorium remains the place most plays are performed, with audiences looking into a picture frame. Theatre spaces are defined below. If you are new to the stage, here's your crash course in the jargon. If not, use it to provide a quick review.

Memorize and master these terms since directors, choreographers, fight directors and movement coaches will use them to block and shape a scene, dance, fight or other stage action.

1. **above** Area away from the audience, upstage
2. **apron** Part of the stage that projects into the auditorium, close to the audience, downstage of the proscenium arch
3. **arena** Form of staging where the audience surrounds the stage on all sides, sometimes called **theatre-in-the-round**
4. **backing** Flats or drops used to mask the backstage area by limiting the audience view through doors, windows or archways on the set
5. **batten** Long pipe or strip of wood on which scenery or drops are hung
6. **below** Toward the audience, downstage
7. **black box** A theatre space with flexible staging and seating, a box that is reconfigured for various productions

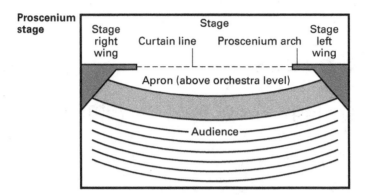

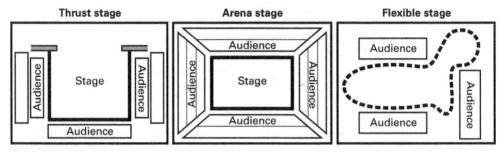

Figure 6.1 Theatre spaces

8. **border** Short curtain hung above the stage, used to mask the flies
9. **box set** Standard set for contemporary, realistic theatre, showing a back wall and two side walls, with the fourth wall understood to be the transparent one through which the audience views the play
10. **callboard** Bulletin board backstage where notes for a show are posted
11. **cyclorama** Curtain or canvas hung at the back of the stage, usually to represent the sky, also called the **cyc**
12. **downstage** Part of the stage nearest the audience
13. **drop** Curtain or flat hung above the stage and dropped or lowered when needed
14. **flat** Single piece of scenery, usually made of muslin, canvas or linen, stretched over a wooden form, used with other similar units to create a set
15. **flies** The area above the stage where curtains, flats and other scenic elements may be stored until it is time to "fly" them down into view
16. **forestage** Part of the stage nearest the audience; *see* **apron**
17. **fourth wall** Imaginary partition through which the audience watches the action
18. **Green Room** Actors' lounge backstage
19. **grid** Framework of wood or steel above the stage, also called **gridiron**
20. **ground plan** Scaled floor plan that shows the ceiling view of the set, including entrances, windows, doors and furniture
21. **house** All areas of the theatre not onstage or backstage: auditorium, lobby, box office, lounges
22. **legs** Flats or curtains at extreme right and left of stage used to mask wings; *see* **tormenters**

23. **mask** To conceal from view of the audience
24. **props** Any articles handled or carried by the actor
25. **proscenium (arch)** Opening through which audience views the stage
26. **rake** To place the floor of any area of the set on a slant; like a ramp
27. **scrim** Net curtain, stretched taut, which can become transparent or opaque depending on how it is lit, so that the audience may or may not be able to see through it
28. **sight lines** Areas of the stage visible to the audience
29. **spill** Light leaks around the edges of a lighting area
30. **stage left** Left side of the stage from the actor's point of view, facing the house
31. **stage right** Right side of the stage from the actor's point of view, facing the house
32. **teaser** Border curtain just upstage and in back of the front curtain
33. **thrust** Form of staging with the audience on three sides of the stage, which is thrust from the fourth side into the house
34. **tormenters** Flats or curtains at the extreme right and left of stage; *see* legs
35. **wings** Left and right offstage areas

Acting Areas

The terrain of the stage is mapped out with the following major areas, where you move on major crosses during the staging of a play (up right, right, down right, up center, center, down center, up left, left, down left, usually designated by their initials). Positions refer to the actor's left. One of the most common directions is to move from one of these nine to another, as in: "Start upright, then slowly make your way to center, float down center and end up down left by the time you end the speech."

Which of these areas are strongest and weakest? Closest to center and closest to the audience is considered the most powerful location, so DC is strongest of all, fully visible and intimate. Because we are trained to read left to right, stage right SR (actor's SL) is considered more compelling than left. These generalizations apply to a neutral stage. Power and focus can be instantly shifted by an actor on a higher level or by lighting placing focus anywhere. Shifts in scenic and lighting elements can change everything.

Up right	Up center	Up left
Right center	Center	Left center
Down right	Down center	Down left

Figure 6.2 Stage areas

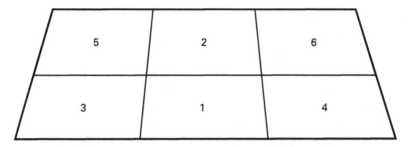

Figure 6.3 Area strengths. The numbers represent the strongest (1) to weakest (6) areas in terms of audience attention.

EXERCISE 6.1 SPACE TRAVEL

Load the terms and locations above into your memory bank, by one or more of the following activities:

1. Visit a theatre and, from a place in the audience area, visually identify each location.
2. Go onstage with the list and move to each spot as you say what and where it is. Go through the list in the order above first, then randomly selecting the next item.
3. If you can work with a partner, take turns with one of you being in the audience and the other onstage.

   Audience partner announce a term and onstage partner move to that location.

4. Make the task more complex by audience partner creating a movement task such as: "Enter from the wings at the second set of legs. Move directly to the cyc, then turn and cross down to the apron."
5. If working with a group, let volunteers shout out instructions, making some effort to build the complexity as the exercise progresses.

Figure 6.4 The crank call. Copyright Hilary B. Price with Stanfill.

Acting Moves

Once you master the locations, there is an additional movement vocabulary for using them. If you have already integrated these into your work, it is worth a quick review to solidify your command of each. A movement is not limited to changing locations, but may simply involve facial expressions, gestures or angling the body in a different way. While some of these are desirable maneuvers, some are distractions, unnoticed by most, to be avoided.

1. **bit** A particularly striking or theatrical piece of business, usually not organically required by the action but added for effect
2. **blocking** Those movements of the actor that are set by the director at some point in the rehearsal process and transcribed into your copy of the text as they are given or solidified
3. **breaking** Dropping character suddenly, often by laughing or in some way "breaking up"
4. **bridge** Transition from one key moment to another, usually in an effort to make a movement appear more natural or spontaneous
5. **business** Pantomimed action with or without props, small movements not involving full stage crosses
6. **cheat** To turn toward the audience while appearing to focus on another player onstage in order to be better seen
7. **closed turn** Turn executed so that the actor turns his back to the audience
8. **composition** Stage picture created by placing actors and properties in various arrangements
9. **counter** Small cross in the opposite direction from a move made by another actor to balance stage composition
10. **cue** Final word, move or technical change that signals you to proceed to your next line or movement
11. **cue to cue** Skipping lengthy passages and running only those moments where change in responsibility occurs, moving from one cue directly to the next
12. **focus** To direct attention toward a focal point so that the audience's attention will follow; you may be asked to give focus to another actor by looking at her and taking a less open position
13. **freeze** To suddenly stand completely still to form a tableau
14. **give stage** To assume a less dominant position in relation to another actor
15. **hold** Any deliberate pause in the play's action
16. **indicating** Showing the audience rather than letting them see; playing actions without intentions
17. **mugging** Exaggerating facial expressions and reactions to the point of caricature
18. **open turn** Turning so that you are always facing the audience during the movement
19. **places** Instruction to take positions which have been set for the beginning of the play or scene
20. **presentational** A way of performing that regularly acknowledges the audience and the theatricality of the event
21. **read** To register with the audience, often used to describe the difference between the way an action feels onstage and the way it actually looks/seems/sounds from the house, also called **play**

22. **representational** Style in which actors create the impression that the audience is not present, that a real-life situation is being represented onstage, so that the audience seems to be eavesdropping
23. **run-through** An uninterrupted rehearsal of the play, an act or scene, in contrast to the stops and starts and repetition that characterize most rehearsals
24. **schtick** Silly or cheap piece of business, usually designed for laughter
25. **share stage** To assume a position of equal importance in relation to another actor
26. **stretch** To take longer to execute something than would normally occur, often done to allow time for a difficult costume or set change
27. **strike** To remove an object from the stage
28. **take** A reaction of surprise, usually involving looking again at the source or the audience; takes may be single, double or triple depending on how many times the look is repeated
29. **take stage** To draw audience attention, to assume a stronger stage position than others, often by moving to a more powerful area or a higher level or by doing something that contrasts strongly with what the other actors are doing
30. **transition** The way you get from one part of the scene or space to another, usually involving some invention of business to facilitate a seamless change

EXERCISE 6.2 **SPACE OWNERSHIP**

The list above is inherently more challenging and varied, yet the same process of loading is useful.

1. While it may be helpful to review these maneuvers on your own in the space at first, the presence of a partner, and ideally a third person to observe from the house, will greatly facilitate the process.
2. Attend a performance with the list in hand and attempt to identify when the actors are executing any of the maneuvers or falling into the patterns above.
3. If you can work with a partner, select a brief scene excerpt and repeat it numerous times with the variations implied by the various moves.
4. Working with a third party or an entire group, take instructions from your audience, such as "Perform the first page in a presentational style, then go back and repeat it in a representational style" or "Start with A taking and B giving focus; when I clap my hands, switch dominance until I do so again."

Stage Pictures

Consider what you communicate at any moment, even in stillness.

Silent Messages

If you and your partner are onstage, before you ever gesture or physically move to another spot or even change the expressions on your faces, an active relationship between the two of you and between each of you and the audience has started.

Two people are onstage. What is going on between them? And perhaps between them and observers? Try each of the following pictures. Ask yourself, what is the impression if:

1. The two of you stand quite close, facing each other, in profile to the audience?
2. Still facing, but with considerable distance between the two of you?
3. Same as 2 but with pieces of furniture actually separating you?
4. You are standing close, but your partner's back is turned to you?
5. You are standing close, but your back is turned to your partner?
6. You are close, but both of you are facing opposite directions?
7. You are standing close, but both of you are facing full front?
8. Both of you are full back?
9. Both of you are one-quarter left or right? Three-quarters left or right?
10. One of you is one-quarter left, the other one-quarter right? You switch?
11. One of you is full front and the other full back?
12. You take any of the close-to-each-other combinations and place it in each of the six major acting areas?
13. You take situation 4, but you are in UR and your partner is DC? The two of you reverse?
14. Any other situation with the two of you in different acting areas?
15. Back to situation 1, but you are both sitting?
16. You are both kneeling?
17. Both of you are on a staircase or ramp? Both up on a platform?
18. Any situation listed, with both of you reclining? Both lying down?
19. Any situation listed so far, with each of you in one of the following positions but always different from each other:

    - on a platform
    - kneeling
    - on a staircase or ramp
    - reclining
    - lying down
    - sitting.

Status – 1 – 5
Standing sitting, laying, improve game

Before even adding business or overt movement, strong messages would have been sent about how open the two characters were to each other and to the audience, about how equal they were, about who was dominant and who subservient, about degrees of power, about barriers to contact and about the relative involvement or indifference of each participant.

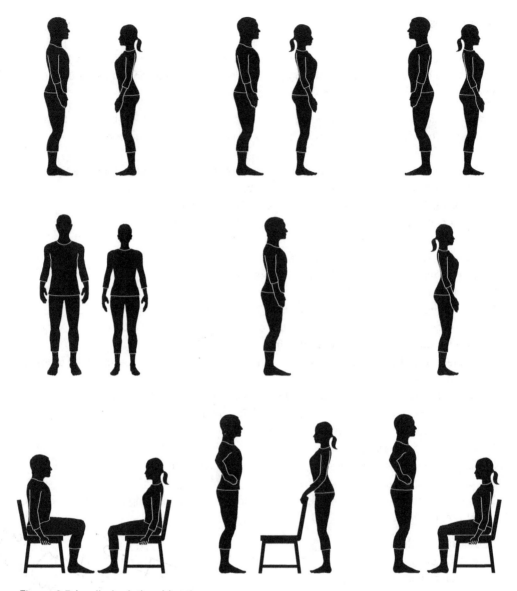

Figure 6.5 Implied relationships

in person

online

EXERCISE 6.3 **AUDIENCE PERSPECTIVE**

1. If working with a group have various sets of two actors take the positions above and discuss the impression with each composition of the implied relationship.
2. If working alone, let a piece of paper represent the stage. Find two small figures of some kind (toy soldiers, chess pieces, standing figures, etc.). Place the figures in each position and attempt to identify the relationship each has created.

3. Put what you see into words, being careful to only identify what the composition actually implies without reading too much that might not actually be there. For example, in situation 1, it is clear that the characters are receptive to or perhaps confrontational with each other, but are not avoiding each other in any way. It is not clear whether the encounter is positive or negative, but it is open.

Moving Pictures

Our first impression can change at once. If the two of you are standing in profile and we cannot hear your conversation, what is the impression if:

1. You are both gesturing with full large bubble, extending arms all the way out and even involving legs in the conversation?
2. You gesture in a normal, everyday range?
3. You gesture in a tight, close-to-the-torso manner?
4. There is any contrast between the two of you in gestural patterns?
5. You both use hand props to emphasize everything you wish to say?
6. One of you uses hand props, but the other does not?
7. You both make long crosses every time you speak?
8. You both make short crosses of just a few feet?
9. One of you moves a great distance and the other a short distance?
10. One of you moves and the other is always still?
11. One of you moves a lot but does not really gesture while the other stands in place but gestures fully?
12. The movements are relatively constant throughout the scene?
13. Large moves come after at least a minute of no movement at all?
14. One of you moves in an erratic, varying pattern while the other is quite predictable?
15. You both tend to move directly and then stop or instead both move to an intermediate location and then change directions before you finally stop? If there is a contrast of directness between you?
16. Your movements tend to be largely pointed straight upstage or downstage?
17. There is constant countering, with moves seeming to go back and forth between the proscenium arch or audience frame?
18. There is a greater use of the diagonal by both or one of you?
19. There is a tendency to circle each other and to move in curves, S shapes or figure eights? If one person uses these circular moves while the other is always heading straight for a target?
20. The movements themselves are rapid and darting?
21. All movements are slow, steady, almost lugubrious?
22. There is a contrast in tempo-rhythms between characters or at various moments in the scene?
23. A movement comes just before a line of text?
24. The line comes first and then the cross?

25. The line is broken, with a movement occurring somewhere in the middle? If one character falls into a movement pattern while the other is quite varied?

There are unlimited combinations of ways to communicate a relationship. The more you practice and observe these maneuvers, the more responsive your body will become to discovering appropriate moves in a more spontaneous way in other contexts. Once you've been exposed consciously to all the ingredients, many simply come to you beyond consciousness when you are exploring within a scene. Many experienced actors advise to learn, integrate and then forget, which really means allowing the knowledge to seep into your subconscious.

EXERCISE 6.4 MOVEMENT MEANINGS

1. When attending a production, if there are moments in the performance that feel off, ask yourself if the shift in relationship you hear from the lines is being appropriately reinforced by movement and if not how it could have been improved.
2. This material is impossible to work solo or with any fewer than three participants and is best served by a group of some size. If this is possible, have everyone memorize a short scene that is relatively neutral in content. An open scene, involving actors 1 and 2, such as these would be ideal:

SHORT OPEN SCENE

1: Oh.
2: So?
1: All set?
2: No.
1: Well.
2: Yes.

1: Forget it.
2: What?
1: Go on.
2: I will.

Each set of partners draws two or three of the movement situations above. Take a few minutes to practice applying the moves with the open dialogue. Then present for the class and discuss the impression made by each shift in movement modality.

Onstage/Offstage Contrasts

Courtesy in life often needs to dissolve for audience attention onstage in order to gain focus. Here are traditional principles, which, while widely followed, are also sometimes violated for effect. On a proscenium stage, you usually:

1. Cross in front of another character, unless that character is seated and you can be seen the whole time.
2. Look at actors who are entering or exiting to help direct attention to them.
3. Move well onto the stage and do not linger when entering. And leave completely.
4. Do not move at the same time as another actor unless momentary chaos is intentional. The audience gets confused about where to look.
5. Move on your own lines and usually remain still on those of other actors.
6. Remain as open to the audience as possible when speaking, with particular awareness of keeping your face, especially your eyes, visible much of the time.
7. Know that if you are standing and the other person is sitting, you will dominate. Though possessing the chair may seem the more powerful and comfortable position, as it often would be offstage, the audience, looking through the picture frame, sees one person looming powerfully over another. Possession is trumped by height. All such assessments of dominance need to be considered as seen through a picture frame.
8. Need to be selective about eye contact. Aim to minimize. Inexperienced actors look at each other not at all or way too much. Actual eye contact has an ebb and flow. In life, it is estimated that real people often look at each other as little as 10% of the time. Even when in a position forcing you to face another person (like a restaurant booth), note how often your eyes dart away or settle on other objects, other diners, memories or to help gather your thoughts. You may return to direct eye contact at the end of such a search or when asked for full attention. When you are in the vast outdoors with a companion, note how seldom the two of you lock eyes and how much of the time you focus on surroundings. In difficult conversations, we often look away for inspiration and survival, and then only return to direct contact when done and ready for a response. Novice actors often stare at partners relentlessly as if this contact is a kind of life line. If there is only one other person in the scene, eye contact tends to be even lower because there is no need to signal to whom your remarks are being directed.
9. In offstage public events, ask yourself if what you may be communicating to those present is intentional. Are you standing further away from your partner than would send an intimate relationship message? Are you accepting or administering hugs in an indiscriminate way? Are you likely to be perceived as you want to be? If not, consider adjusting your focus and behavior. And it never hurts to remember that Shakespeare's statement "all the world's a stage" is more true than ever now that anything you do could be filmed and go viral.

EXERCISE 6.5 **OFFSTAGE TO ON**

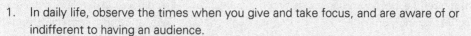

1. In daily life, observe the times when you give and take focus, and are aware of or indifferent to having an audience.
2. Transform these experiences as they would be observed onstage. What would change as a result of being viewed from the house or a similar distance?
3. On a regular basis, after an experience onstage or off, ask yourself how it would have seemed different for the presence or absence of a fourth wall.

Self-Staging

All the elements in this chapter are of particular interest to directors who are ultimately responsible for the staging of a show. Why then not simply leave such matters to them? Because the more you know, the more you can contribute to the process, enhancing movements and coming up with creative alternatives. You want sufficient staging savvy to be an active collaborator.

Some directors do not pre-block plays but rather stage them organically, meaning they encourage actors to explore the space and then try to select the most interesting of these explorations and discoveries made throughout the rehearsal period. In such instances the staging is not set until very late in the process. Clearly the more you have mastered the material above, the better the explorer you will be.

Some directors lack staging skills and are therefore very dependent on their actors to create interesting stage pictures. In these instances your knowledge becomes a survival skill. Remember, the director can always leave town after opening night. You are the one who has to go out there over and over, hopefully in ways that are clear, fluid and compelling.

There are also instances, such as preparing for an audition or to present a scene in class, where you do not have someone else to monitor staging and are largely on your own. Even if you have access to a coach or can call upon classmates to observe and give you feedback before actually presenting the work, you do not want to encounter auditioners clueless, with no sense of how you might use the space to tell your character's story. Again, the more you bring, the more you are likely to get.

Be open, responsive and grateful for any movement input from others, while knowing that if it comes down to it you will be able to stage yourself.

Arena and Thrust Self-Staging

Self-staging in these spaces is an almost impossible proposition. Take great care to not get involved in a show in one of them without a director known and admired for staging skill.

The proscenium arch is like a picture frame and the audience only ever gets the side (1/4 of possibilities) seen through that frame. This makes it easy for you to take a position and create a stage picture with a relatively clear sense of what those looking through the arch will see. However, in thrust, audiences sit on three sides of the stage and in arena on all four. Some of them will be very close to the acting area and entirely visible to you because of inevitable light spill into the seating areas. They can seem to be breathing down your neck. Their close proximity and visibility make them immediately present and potentially distracting. You are scrutinized far beyond proscenium circumstances. And all audiences get a different view of you; at any moment one audience member will see your face, another your behind, another your profile and various alternatives. You need to act with your whole self because that is how you are being observed, albeit some part of yourself different to each of them.

Self-Staging for Film

Ironically, one of the greatest challenges of movement mastery for the screen is learning how to not move at all. You may need to be far more still than your own tendencies in real life because tiny mannerisms and minuscule movement can be amplified to the point of distraction.

> *On my first film, another actor said "Come watch the playback". Thank God she did! My eyebrows kept moving way up and I was acting to the back of the room. Suddenly I realized why I'd never gotten a film job before.*
>
> **Eddie Redmayne, actor**

What is often required is not simple lack of motion, but rather dynamic stillness. There needs to be a great deal going on inside you. Stage acting is sometimes described as finding the right activity, while film is about finding the right thoughts or feelings and then just letting the camera in. Film actors are often advised to just "be" because anything more can be too much.

Because much of the "staging" will be done by the camera, as it changes angles and distances, you will wish to find out where it will be and what is the shot. There are seven basic ones, moving from great distance to practically under your skin.

1. *Distant—Extreme long shot.* The camera feels remote and almost indifferent.
2. *Public—Long shot.* The shot is more than 12 feet and relatively impersonal. Also called a full shot—all of your body, head to toe.
3. *Formal Social—Medium shot.* Camera is 8 to 12 feet from you, the distance in many casual or business encounters. We can see much of your torso, probably above the knees.
4. *Familiar Social—Medium close shot.* 4 to 8 feet, cutting you off just below the waist, putting more emphasis on facial expressions.
5. *Personal—Close shot.* One and a half to four feet away, shot cuts you off at the collarbone or chest and begins to allow us into your inner life.
6. *Intimate—Close up.* Only your head and neck are in the frame. Subtext becomes as important as text. Used for reaction shots, discoveries and important moments of realization or change.
7. *Internal—Extreme close up.* Even closer than intimate. Only your face or part of it is onscreen. For powerful, high-emotion moments.

A skilled screen actor may rely heavily on using public solitude to shut out all the whirling studio or location activity and be completely in the moment, particularly as these shots move closer.

> *The lens has psychic strength. The camera can see beneath the skin.*
>
> **Martin Scorsese, director**

Screen performers are often expected to move closer to other actors and props beyond normal everyday interaction because the camera creates space. In stage acting, we are frequently asked to cheat out to the audience, but cheating is used in film as well with very distinct conventions. You are likely to be expected:

1. *Moves:* To slow down whatever you are doing to give the camera operator warning to shift and follow you. You must usually make crosses slightly more slowly than in life; the same will be true for rising from a chair, including a bit more preparation before you do so. In movements with props, such as picking up a glass or answering the phone, you are generally expected to linger just a bit longer than you might in life as you grasp the prop before you pick it up and then to make the movement itself less rapidly.

2. *Eyes:* To cheat just your eyes. If you are in a shot where your partner's back is to the camera and your face is in focus, you may be asked to look into just one of your partner's eyes—the one closest to the camera to keep your eyes more open to it. This is called "eye-line."

3. *Position:* To fill the empty space between actors which the camera absolutely hates. It tends to exaggerate this gap, making the two of them seem miles apart when they are actually in normal proximity. Not only are you likely to move much closer to your partner than you would normally be in life, but you may actually be pressing against the other person bodily so that your heads can appear to be in a normal relationship onscreen.

If you watch dailies, you may determine where any of the adjustments above would improve your work, even if you have not been asked to make them, which would up your game. It is important to grow comfortable with these conventions and the more knowledge you have of what the camera will be filming, the more competent you will feel.

Circles of Concentration

The legendary acting innovator Stanislavski invented a tool to assist in all of the pressures and challenges above. His Circles of Concentration (sometimes called Circles of Attention) offer a way of working the audience in and out of your consciousness as necessary. Distractions, such as an audience member coughing loudly or laughing at a totally unexpected place, a loud backstage noise or a misplaced prop, are just a few of the potential disturbances that can take you out of the moment and break your performance concentration. When you feel yourself becoming distracted, narrow your Circle of Attention to the smallest possible immediate space around you to momentarily collect yourself.

1. You focus on a specific task right in front of you whenever you feel your concentration or involvement wavering. The more minute and physical the task, the better—writing, cleaning your glasses, picking a thread off your coat sleeve, searching within a book, etc. Giving your entire attention to a very specific hand prop or part of your costume or the pattern in the upholstery fabric on your chair are common narrow circle actions. It is as if you are alone, though observed. Stanislavski calls this "public solitude."

2. You spiral out your circle to include your acting partner when the two of you need to interact and you feel sufficiently collected to do so. The circle surrounds the two of you and yet excludes the rest of the world.

3. You spiral out further to include the entire stage at the appropriate moment when your character's focus should expand to the acting space as a whole.

4. You spiral yet further to take in the audience when there is a specific audience response

to deal with, such as holding for a laugh or any other challenge of "playing the house," when the timing of a moment is of the utmost importance and a sense of how observers are responding is crucial.

These circles keep widening and narrowing according to the needs of the moment. Stanislavski has described them as "elastic," letting the actor's awareness stretch, expand and contract with minimal effort as needed. Circles may also be used for more than distractions. For example, there are acting physical tasks where you are more or less secure. A dance number may have stretches where your confidence allows you to use your largest all inclusive circle, other stretches where the technical challenge is so difficult that you have never gotten beyond a very small circle ("Step, ball, change, pivot, repeat" you may be saying silently to yourself). Your circles will fluctuate accordingly.

You may decide to move between the four circles, not just to deal with distraction or insecurity, but simply to weave a textured and multilayered performance. An audience can be quite mesmerized by moments of public solitude because they feel as if they are eavesdropping on the character's privacy. Your circle choices will also be influenced by the size of the theatre and audience, with the most narrow easiest in small, intimate spaces and the largest often needed for playing large auditoriums and amphitheatres.

As an actor, you do not wish to be obsessed with the audience. But you wish to have at your disposal the means of widening and narrowing your perception because, as Stanislavski says, "the audience constitutes the spiritual acoustics for us. They give back what they receive from us as living, human emotions."

Method of Physical Actions

A second major gift from Stanislavski for achieving a state in which you can perform persuasively for an audience is his Method of Physical Actions, which allows the discovery of strong movements in rehearsal which continue in performance.

This Method is based on three propositions:

1. You need to achieve a state that is like a normal person in life. To do this, you must be physically free and controlled, alert and attentive, listening and observing, as well as believing—that is able to live convincingly inside the reality of the character.
2. If you put yourself in the place of the character, you will achieve honest action onstage by combining psychological action (strong motives) and physical action (expressing these motives through sustained and expressive movement).
3. The organic action resulting from this combination will produce (if you have thoroughly researched and analyzed the role) sincere, believable feelings.

The wonderful part of the Method of Physical Actions is the way the ingredients sustain each other in a symbiotic relationship. If, for example, you achieve a state of angry frustration and forcefully grab the back of a chair, the movement is just right and you may never have discovered it without immersing yourself in the character's perspective. In performance, even if you are not always fully angry, the power of the move, as the body remembers it and anticipates it, is likely to help you generate anger and consistently communicate it to an audience. Even on an off night, your action is so strong that it will read convincingly. Stanislavski understood that the body was more directly reliable and available than the emotions, which "run through your fingers like water," and that the body should therefore be used as a pathway to elusive feelings.

Summary

This chapter has provided you with the core vocabulary for being in a theatre space and moving there. We have reviewed terms associated with theatre geography along with tips for reading the map and navigating the areas, including the relative strength of stage positions. Specific acting moves have been identified, including changing locations, facial expressions, gestures or angling the body, some more and some less desirable, but all important to recognize. Next, the impact of various stage compositions has been explored, first in stillness and then with the addition of motion. You have been educated in the ways in which movement etiquette onstage differs from that in daily life. Your need to master self-staging, in varying spaces and when filming, as a simple survival mechanism as well as a communicative tool has been established. Your use of the Circles of Concentration and the Method of Physical Actions will greatly aid your focus and control. You should now feel prepared to take part in rehearsal as an active and informed participant, ready to collaborate.

CHAPTER 7 ACTING STYLES

Acting Styles

Using information from the worlds of nonrealistic plays to develop believable style characterizations

The amazing thing about classical theatre is how much of your work has already been done for you. It is right there in the script.

Christopher Plummer, actor

When you play a king, the first important thing to remember is that when you walk into a room, everything around you, you own.

Keith Mitchell, actor

In realistic theatre, actors are often cast close to age and type. Behavior is familiar. This is our dominant style. Any time a show moves away from realism, it is called "stylized" or is described as done in "the Fill-in-the-Blank Style." You stylize an event by removing it from everyday expected demeanor and conduct. The more boldly stylized a production, the more conventions or rules of make-believe the audience must accept, in order to engage and appreciate it.

New Worlds

For an actor, style work involves a journey outside of known territory. This often involves changing yourself enough to believably enter another world, formerly unfamiliar to you or to most audiences. The same outside the theatre, where you are thought of as having real style if you can move with relative ease between worlds.

Our two most popular stylized forms are musical theatre, where characters can break into song and dance at any moment, and Shakespeare, where they often break into poetic, elevated verse and swordplay, not exactly the behavior of the people down the block.

Here are some of the new worlds you may be asked to enter:

- **Nonrealistic modern drama**, sometimes called **ISMs** for the final syllable in most of their titles include the following in the order in which they first emerged: Romanticism early 1800s, Realism 1850s, Naturalism 1873, Impressionism 1874, Symbolism 1890–1920, Expressionism 1910, Futurism 1910–1930, Dadaism 1916, Constructivism 1921, Surrealism 1924, Didacticism 1927, Absurdism late 1940s, Feminism late 1960s, Postmodernism 1980s.
- **Period style** is the term most often used for classical plays that have survived through the ages. Because these were the moments when drama rose to its highest potential, plays from these periods are often revived. They most often include: Ancient Greece (5th–3rd centuries BCE), Elizabethan England (1580–1620, most notably Shakespeare), Neoclassic (France mid- to late 1600s, largely Molière), The Restoration (England late 1600s) and Georgian (late 1700s) periods. Displaced plays are style blends, where a play is set in one era, written in another and perhaps performed in a third, so all eras involved need to be researched and blended.
- **Musical theatre** may involve a variety of subgenres: Concept musicals, Rock, African American, Family, Jukebox, Mega, Sing-Through and Postmodern musicals. Each has distinct conventions beyond song and dance for establishing a world.
- **Unexpected contexts and combinations** may incorporate existing forms in entirely new ways. Some shows may be presented in a style altogether different from that for which the script was written. This is particularly true with Asian forms, such as Kabuki and Noh, as well as the use of Bunraku style puppets and masks as conventions incorporated into Western plays, as productions blend or fuse styles in new ways.

Because acting style is a subject requiring study all on its own outside the context of this text, we cannot cover all the conventions for all the stylized events listed above. We can provide you with key questions to ask as you approach each play or world. The great temptation is to look at the physical behavior first (they hold their pinkies thus, they sweep off their hats in greeting, they bow or curtsey deeply) without finding the organic source of that choice. It is tempting to load from the outside in terms of movement. You need to attack this world with the same vigor and insatiable curiosity characteristic of an anthropologist entering a new territory, trying to figure out what it feels like to live there.

Engaging the Style Checklist

The World of the Play list in Chapter 5 becomes even more important when you are in a classical period style piece because the world is so different from the one in which you lead your day to day existence. To enter this entirely new world you need even more so to understand about the sense of time, space, place, values, structure, beauty, sex, recreation and how these are manifested through sight and sound for those who live there.

Here is a review of that list. Ask:

Time—Tempo/rhythm? Age? Point in history?
Space—Bubbles? Privacy? Invasion?
Place—Setting? Relationship to nature? Awareness of others?

Values—Mood? Ideals? Money? God? Emotion?
Structure—Government? Daily life? Education?
Beauty—Looks? Comfort? Artistic expression?
Sex—Expression? Seduction? Courtship?
Recreation— Occasions? Participation? Consumption?
Sight—Stillness? Movement? Ritual?
Sound—Language? Listening? Music?

If any of these categories do not appear immediately clear, review Chapter 5, pp. 112–114, where they are explained in some detail.

Research

So how do you answer these questions?

1. An amazing amount of answers are in the script itself if you examine it with this list by your side, which will make for a much deeper reading of the text than staying at plot level. And the answers will be different, for example, from one Shakespeare script to another, because he creates a new universe each time.
2. Study the artifacts of the period in which the play was written: paintings, sculptures, architecture, music (including favored instruments and musical forms), clothing, hairstyles and perhaps most important popular dances, because the way partners interact reveal a great deal about relationships within the culture.
3. Examine renderings of theatre spaces for a sense of environment, size, atmosphere and proximity between actors and audiences.
4. Histories, particularly letters and diaries of the period, can be revealing, though remember that you want to enter the world of the playwright's imagination, which may be quite different from the one in which he actually lived.
5. As suggested in Chapter 5, use the considerable knowledge and expertise of your dramaturge.
6. Make use of the acting style texts identified in Chapter 8, which can offer detailed information and illustrations on social interaction through bows, curtseys, the use of capes, fans, masks, farthingales and myriad other accoutrements.

While we cannot cover all styles, classical acting is such a prevailing challenge that we will examine it here and offer guidelines for you to take crucial questions into other worlds.

Period Style Actors

What makes an actor classical? Robert conducted an extensive survey in which actors were asked to list well known other actors, all of whom they admired, but to place some as potentially classical (A list) and others as not (B), with a brief explanation of the qualities that either encouraged or discouraged inclusion in the classical designation. Those chosen included the words poise—grace—class—power—sophistication—presence—versatility—voice—boldness—size—sensitivity—eloquence—depth—control—command—stature—intensity—focus—clarity—mystery—universality—majesty. Those admired for their acting generally, but not regarded as classical (B list), often involved the preposition **too**, followed by: limited—rough—flat—low class—conventional—shallow—comedic—crude—small—light—ethnic—informal—slow—contemporary—insensitive—weak—subdued—simple—monotonous—internal—awkward.

EXERCISE 7.1 **EMBRACING YOUR "A"**

1. Either read the B list of words out loud yourself or have a group member do so while you and others allow those same words to encompass you. Allow yourself to move or freeze in a way that really manifests the word and makes you feel very much like a person with those qualities and characteristics.

2. Take a moment to shake all of those out and return to a highly receptive neutral.

3. Do the same with the A list words, letting each envelop your entire being and allowing the authority and confidence to seep into your bones.

4. Select three A words in particular that seem truly evocative and allow you to embrace a classical version of yourself. Use these when you need to let go of your B and embrace your A persona.

Dressing for Success
1558–1603

Figure 7.1 Dressing for success. Copyright F. Eino.

While hilarious, the cartoon in Figure 7.1, based on portraits of Queen Elizabeth I, is not as exaggerated as you might imagine. Go to those original paintings and allow yourself to be stunned by the sheer overwhelming scale of her garments, wig, jewelry and props. She and her courtiers entered the world each day taking up an enormous amount of space, a reflection of the Elizabethan huge sense of self as larger than life and exuding extraordinary confidence. Aside from the challenge of learning to command such a costume, to wear it and not allow it to wear and overwhelm you, you need to embrace the sheer belief in self that it takes to pull it all off.

Common Classical Threads

Actors who are classic chameleons can take us back in history or forward into fantasy. While not excusing you from a deep script analysis, there are likelihoods:

Time—moves less predictably, veering wildly between breathtaking speed and the careful consideration of an idea. Because it is set "ago," it rejects scientific inquiry in favor of miracles as a way to explain life.

Space—is larger. Your concept of self radiates and flashes. You fill a void when you enter. The invasion of another's space is more likely to be direct and sudden (as in sweeping someone into your arms and kissing them or boldly striking an opponent) with less hesitation and sneaking around. Space is there to be taken.

Place—is both grander and simpler. You may be in the palace, forest, temple, battlefield or public square. You may be on an island or mountain top. A more mundane spot, such as a drawing room, is merely suggested. You are less likely to have something to lean on, sit on or play with. You are far more likely to occasionally acknowledge the presence of the audience. The place will change more by your imagination than scenic devices.

Values—involve following one's own destiny which is often also the destiny of others, so your acts have great consequences. History is important and the divine rights of monarchs more revered. No one holds attention without speaking well. Life is to be lived fully and forcefully, even in sin and error, not acted safely and softly.

Structure—means order comes from stars and fates. Who you are when you are born is vital to who you will be when you die. Rulers (in country and family) are less often questioned. You play by rules or you change them, often the latter.

Beauty—is more abstract, the *expression* of it even more rewarded than the *possession* of it. You create beauty in your speech and create yourself when you go into the world. You handle far more fabric and accoutrements and it helps to have features strong enough to match the clothes.

Sex—does not hide or cower. At times it drops from consideration because issues at hand are so much more significant. At others, it is the meaning of life. In general it is dealt with more frankly and enthusiastically, with less giggles or embarrassment.

Recreation—often involves public celebrations. Shyness is less tolerated. Life is a banquet. Capacity to overindulge is more tolerated, even honored. Each person is expected to contribute to the event, to make the party happen.

Sight and Sound—involve greater contrasts. Stillness and economy are interrupted with bursts of physical boldness. You are able to do absolutely nothing and pull listeners into your consciousness. You are also able to reach out to the back of the theatre and embrace everyone there in your energy and power. Clear, crisp, clean speech gives maximum attention to consonants. You are able to speak at length with complexity and authority.

Note that in almost all periods prior to the twentieth century, a significantly larger human silhouette exists with particular needs to master the way capes, sleeves, skirts influence posture and movement, requiring considerable preparation on the part of the actor to achieve mastery.

Figure 7.2 Clothing through time

What follows are the areas where young actors in classical plays are asked to make adjustments.

Special Skills

There are some common actor tasks which rarely exist in realistic theatre but must become absolutely comfortable for an actor in the classics:

1. *Asides*—right in the middle of a scene, one character turns to the audience to confide in them, ask them a question, give them a knowing look or in some other way quickly connect with them before returning to the scene. These are sharp clicks. Keep your body facing the direction it was going and simply snap your head out to face the audience, especially if the aside is very brief. If it is longer or more pronounced, try leaning sharply toward the audience. To punch it up one step more, dash quickly downstage to confide in us, then dash back to where you were and continue as if nothing has happened. Partners of actors doing asides need to look *away* at the moment of the aside to help the illusion. They need to find something to occupy them, go into slow motion or freeze. Never watch the actor doing the aside. Help create the impression that, from your perspective, it never happened.

EXERCISE 7.2 SCENE FULL OF ASIDES

Use this scene to master all three forms of asides. If working in a group, have each pair present, discuss, and have another pair try it until there is a general feeling of mastery. (A and B enter from opposite sides of the stage.)

> A: Ah, it's so delightful to see you.
> B: And you, my dear.
> (aside) My God, she looks like death warmed over.
> And how is your love life?
> A: Oh, divine. Superb. Unparalleled.
> (aside) Not that it's really any of the little twit's business.
> B: I'm delighted to hear it!
> (aside) And I don't believe a word of it.
> We must dine together soon.
> A: Yes, we simply must!
> (aside) I'd rather die than dine with this imbecile.
> B: I must run.
> A: (aside) Yes, please run as far away as possible.
> B: Bye Bye.
> A: Ta Ta. See you soon
> (A exits).
> B: (aside) Or when hell freezes over. (exits)

Figure 7.3 Classical conventions: John Tufts and the Oregon Shakespeare Festival ensemble. Classical theatre involves highly stylized movement sequences where the audience is addressed directly. Copyright photographer Jenny Graham.

2. *Audience address*—with perhaps only one character onstage. Most soliloquys work best as direct address rather than an attempt at deep introspective talking out loud to yourself. Because the plays move back and forth between overt acknowledgement of and ignoring your listeners, think of the audience as your collective best friend and confidant, always welcoming your contact but never demanding it. You have the most open, sharing and honest relationship you have with anyone. No one ever lies in a soliloquy. Alone with the audience you speak the absolute truth (as you see it) and without embarrassment.

3. *Rehearsal garments*—are fundamental to get the feel of costumes to come. If they are not available, create them out of your closet or off your bed. Most characters handle a lot more cloth than we do. Capes, trains, lengthy sleeves, elaborate head dresses, trailing ribbons, lace, petticoats—each age is different but the garment is always challenging. *Wear* these and do not let them wear you. Flip them out of the way. Command them. You have a lot of fabric because you deserve it. Dominate it. When wearing a floor length gown or robe, expend as little effort to lift the hem as possible. Use just one hand and lift it only a few inches from the ground when you climb a staircase. You don't need to lift it at all when you descend a staircase. Recognize in each instance, how little effort is needed to command the clothes.

4. *Invented ritualized contact*—showing signs of respect, exorcising demons, calling on the gods, pleading for help, begging for mercy, handing someone the message from an oracle, maneuvers where we have no evidence to prove how they were done back then. Answers emerge in improvisation, trial and error. Let the character show you how he wants these rituals performed.

5. *Handling weapons*—the capacity to believably wear them, carry them and fight well with them is important to the classical actor. It is essential to start early and work actively outside rehearsal. Just achieving enough finesse to make sure the sword at your side is worn with grace and does not stick into you or someone else requires time. Combat scenes are rehearsed twenty times as much as any stretch of dialogue. Basic sword fight principles:

1. Often, a fight is a scene about two people trying to kill each other. Remember, it is a scene at heart, with objectives and evaluations.
2. The pauses where nothing happens are often the most interesting, besides giving you a break.
3. There are only five basic cuts (attack moves) and parries (defense) moves in most sword fights, which are then repeated in limitless combinations. They are not difficult to learn and fights are less complex than they seem at first glance.
4. The blows themselves break down into three distinct parts: the wind-up (size and speed show the audience how strong the blow is), hit (with a split second pause after) and reaction or follow-through (which shows how hard the blow struck or took).
5. Each stage is helped by nonverbal orchestration (grunts, howls, blades clashing, gasps, observer reactions, etc.) and the blow is the least important part. The clear signals are sent by wind-up and reaction. Do not be intimidated from the great fun of getting to die and kill without consequences. While you need to work with a strong fight coach, this skill is highly learnable.

Figure 7.4 Stage combat

EXERCISE 7.3 NLP/VAK LABAN

Style acting often demands strong and vivid choices. Laban's effort actions (see Chapter 4) offer you impulses to really go for it. The essential elements (Visual, Auditory, Kinesthetic or VAK) of Neuro Linguistic Programming (NLP, see p. 78) offer a way to master these quickly and to place them in your working repertoire. Review of basic concepts:

LABAN ACTIONS:

Making an effort that is:

1. **Press** Direct, Slow, Strong
2. **Glide** Direct, Slow, Light
3. **Punch** Direct, Quick, Strong
4. **Dab** Direct, Quick, Light
5. **Wring** Indirect, Slow, Strong
6. **Float** Indirect, Slow, Light
7. **Slash** Indirect, Quick, Strong
8. **Flick** Indirect, Quick, Light

NLP MODALITIES:

Experiencing an event as:

Visual: pictures, films, charts, screens (color below)
Auditory: conversation, music, noise (line)
Kinesthetic: feelings, physical and psychological (action)

- If you are working alone, review the effort itself, then the color, action and line of dialogue, then get up and enact it as fully as possible. Repeat each of the components out loud to help load them into your memory.
- If you are in a class or cast, stand in a circle around the teacher/director with everyone facing outward. As the guide reads the description, allow yourself to embrace those elements, then move outward performing the action while saying the line. After each effort action return to the tight circle again, ready for the next.

1. **Press** Direct, Slow, Strong

   Color—murky dark grey

   Action—trying to move an impossibly large, heavy boulder

   Line—"I've GOT . . . to MOVE this thing . . . but it won't BUDGE!!"

2. **Glide** Direct, Slow, Light

   Color—pale pink chiffon

Action—removing a flower from behind your back, stepping forward and presenting it

Line—"And this, my darling, is for you."

3. **Punch** Direct, Quick, Strong

Color—black exploding into red

Action—punching an adversary in the face and chest over and over

Line—"Take THAT you BASTARD! And THAT! And THAT! AND THIS!!!!!"

4. **Dab** Direct, Quick, Light

Color—bright yellow

Action—Using a brush to put the final touches on a painting

Line—"It needs a touch of color . . . there! And there. And right *there*!"

5. **Wring** Indirect, Slow, Strong

Color—dull greens, olive, pea green, military green

Action—writhing while rubbing hands and lower arms

Line—"Dear God it hurts. Oh please, please let it stop. I need . . . must have . . . release. Some peace! Please!"

6. **Float** Indirect, Slow, Light

Color—various extremely pale pastels

Action—swaying back and forth with weight shifting very lightly from one foot to the other, arms swinging gracefully

Line—"I feel so light! I am a reed shifting in the breeze. I am mist, I am gauze, I am air!"

7. **Slash** Indirect, Quick, Strong

Color—brown mud in heavy rain

Action—swinging a two handed broadsword side to side at all levels against unseen attackers

Line—"Get away! Get off me! Fuck off! Get lost! Get off!!!"

8. **Flick** Indirect, Quick, Light

Color—flashes of Day-glo yellow and green

Action—taunting and tickling

Line—"Are you ticklish? Are you? Are you? Hmmm? Hmmm? Thought so! Ticky, ticky, ticky!!"

Film Style and Scale

For the most part, film acting involves greater restraint and subtlety than stage work, just as realistic/naturalistic scripts are likely to require smaller choices than grand period style pieces. Unfortunately, taking it down for screen close-ups involves a series of don'ts: don't fidget, don't blink much, don't look down much, don't move your hand or props in and out of the frame, don't do sudden, surprising moves, don't shift your weight. Lowering scale can therefore risk becoming lifeless instead of alive with nuance. Instead of fearfully avoiding these distractions, decide that you do not *need* them. Channel the energy that might normally be defused in any of them into really looking, listening and feeling. Let the camera read your mind. The phrase "still waters run deep" is never more true than with effective film acting. Let yours run deep.

As an actor you want the facility to recognize what is needed and then to go as big or small as needed. Scale presents a particular challenge for technique and truth. How does one manage to be much bigger or much smaller and still seem real? Start inside by going deeper into the character for motives that will make a large or small performance inevitable and therefore both easy and believable. When large scale works, it is often because the character is so full of the joy of life that his exuberance is not forced but is simply an expression of who this person is. Or so full of resentment, envy, passion, frustrated boredom or fury that no small behavior would express the urgency the character feels within. If you can find an inner state to allow a larger response to the world, scale adjustment is more likely to come naturally, without self-conscious effort. If you can find a powerful inner truth, much of your outer technique will fall into place. Small often involves someone with all those impulses suppressed, but bubbling under the surface.

How do you adjust? As a film actor, make sure you know the exact context of the section being filmed and the nature of the shot. As a stage actor, whenever you enter a room, size it up. Stage acting guidelines should transfer to other public presentations of self, including giving a speech, making a report, being interviewed, chairing a meeting, reading a press release in public or any context in which you are performing for an audience in a space that is not necessarily one in which you prepared. In all performance contexts, notice how far you are from the back wall, where your primary observers are and how many there are. If you get a chance, practice to see how much sound and physical energy it takes to fill this space without overwhelming it. Identify differences between where you practiced and where you are now. Actors who tour regularly often get to know the hall they will play in tonight by throwing lines out to the back wall; even playing catch with sound. If you can get into the space alone (or better yet with a friend to help you gauge appropriate scale), use that chance. If others go before you, note carefully which of them adequately fills the space and how. Note if any either overwhelm the room or fail to occupy it fully. What adjustments should they have made?

If a performance is scaled large, it may be called "over the top" or "larger than life." These are not necessarily insults because they may be either expressions of gratitude for a bravura piece of work or a statement of reservations about scale appropriateness. A performance scaled small may be dismissed as dull, inadequate or lackluster, or praised for its depth, subtlety and nuance. The key is knowing the right time to make the right scale choice and how to do it.

Offstage Scale

We need to adjust the acting of our lives to our surroundings, but some of us have no space sense. Ask yourself what kind of energy the room, the group or a single listener may need from you. This awareness can start with a few simple scale observations:

1. Who are the largest- and smallest-scaled persons you know?
2. Who is strongest at adjusting to various circumstances?
3. Who is the weakest at noticing or making any effort?
4. Are there circumstances in which you are more or less likely to forget to make adjustments yourself?

Once you answer these questions, your style radar should be vastly improved. Continue to observe scale choices and learn from them.

Summary

Style acting amounts to transporting the audience and yourself into unfamiliar territory, which may involve another era, country, realm or imaginary universe. The most common of these are the ISMs, period styles, musical theatre and mix or fusion blends. Entry should involve analyzing time, space, place, values, structure, beauty, sex, recreation, sight and sound represented in each play, along with considerable research. All classical roles share some similar characteristics and require mastery of specific techniques. Adjusting the scale of performance is a crucial skill for film, varying sized theatre spaces and numerous offstage contexts.

CHAPTER 8 MOVEMENT FUTURE

Movement Future

Continuing to grow as a performer

All the study and work came together in a way that was quite thrilling.

Eddie Redmayne, actor

Because I didn't know anything, I was very specific and extensive in my research. Then I had to apply it.

Julianne Moore, actor

Role Models

The opening quotes in this chapter are about two of the most highly honored film perfor-mances of the past decade, best acting Academy Award winners Eddie Redmayne for *The Theory of Everything* and Julianne Moore for *Still Alice*, who largely swept every other major award on their way to Oscars. Both actors played characters with overwhelming debilitating illnesses, where we first meet them in the very light initial stages of the condition and then experience its devastating increase and subsequent consequences. So the actors needed to take the audience on the full journey of the illness. Here are insights into how they did it.

(From *Interview* magazine, where he is questioned by Jennifer Lawrence)

REDMAYNE: *For this film, I had to watch the dailies, because we were jumping in and out of all these different time periods and trying to track the illness and the physical decline. I had an iPad with all the documentary footage of Stephen [Hawking] and then we had the dailies. I kept hoping that the two things were going to meet, but obviously they never did.* [laughs]

LAWRENCE: *What was your most helpful tool? Was it the Stephen documentaries?*

REDMAYNE: *There was one documentary of Stephen and [exwife] Jane from the 1980s. It's the only footage I could find of Stephen speaking, and he's almost incomprehensible. The illness has really taken hold of his physicality. He can still move, but it was a very specific*

Figure 8.1 Eddie Redmayne.
Copyright Nickon.

physicality. You could still see the mischief in him, the glint in his eye. I had these three images in my trailer—one was Einstein with his tongue out, another was James Dean, because Stephen is just effortlessly cool. He has this kind of shambolic confidence to him. And the last one was a joker in a pack of cards, a marionette with a puppet, because when you meet Stephen—I describe it as a "Lord of Misrule" quality—he's got a great sense of mischief.

I worked with a dancer as well, an amazing woman called Alex Reynolds. My instinct was to try to learn the different stages of the physicality like a dance. Like learning steps, you never have a hold of it—I'm a shit dancer by the way—but once you know the steps, you can then play. So we went to these ALS [amyotrophic lateral sclerosis] clinics in London to become educated in the specifics of the disease. Then I'd go to a studio and Alex would film me walking with a dropped foot or something, and we would go and scrutinize it. It's one of the things that you can't see on your own. The other thing about ALS is that no one knows when it starts. You normally discover you've got it because you fall and go to the ER, and they'll just bandage you up and send you home. It takes a really astute doctor to realize that the reason you fell was because your foot muscle has dropped. I take it that Stephen probably already had ALS from the outset of the film, so I tried to find the little details in his hands and stuff that Alex would just be rigorous with. And you know how quite often people don't understand how actors work and so they treat us with kid gloves?

LAWRENCE: *Yeah, like a land mine.*

REDMAYNE: *Well, she came from the world of dance and she was like, "Do it again! Keep doing it, keep doing it!" Which was just what I needed.*

Figure 8.2 Julianne Moore. Copyright David Shankbone.

(From an interview in the *Philadelphia Inquirer* by Stephen Rea)

MOORE: *I'm very fortunate that Alzheimer's hasn't been something that I've had close experience with either family or friends, which is unusual . . . But because I didn't know anything, I was very specific and extensive in my research. I didn't want to represent anything on screen that I hadn't seen. So I dove in, meeting with clinicians, researchers, and neuro-psychiatrists . . . I sat in on support groups, and visited facilities where I spoke with caregivers, family members and patients. I did Skype calls with women around the country who had been diagnosed with Early-Onset Alzheimer's, what they call younger-onset . . . And one of the women I spoke to said a beautiful thing. She learned that she was not the most reliable narrator of her own life . . . And that's how we experience our own lives—we are our reference point, we're our own narrators, but then we're not.*

If you take nothing else away from this chapter, let it be that you will promise that your research and rehearsal regarding the physical life of any character you play will always be on a par with theirs. You may never reach their level of skill or acclaim, but you can achieve a point where you can say that you did everything in your power to honor every movement, every moment of stillness, every use of your body in the service of a complete, detailed and honest performance. Earlier chapters provide you with guidelines for doing your homework and then for applying it physically. Let this launch you.

Regular Practice

For the immediate future, devise your own program to achieve and then keep your body tuned and ready for movement challenges. Over the course of the text we have identified these areas as those contributing to movement mastery:

1. aerobics
2. strength
3. flexibility
4. focus
5. coordination
6. composure
7. physical imagination

There are numerous activities focusing on growth in each of these seven areas. Now is the time to select a favorite for each and to integrate them into a regular routine. It is far less important which activities you are engaging than that you are engaged. If there is a period where you are not enrolled in movement classes or involved in a production which incorporates movement training and conditioning, keep this list active in your life. Stay in touch with your total physical being so that when the chance to return to class arrives, you will be tuned and ready.

Figure 8.3 Treadmill Grim Reaper. Copyright Joedator.

Tangential Areas of Study

These disciplines can offer strong support for your basic theatre movement training. If they are not offered in your program, they probably are elsewhere on campus or in your community.

Dance—Actors are often taking some kind of dance class, not just for the skills imparted but because it is one of the best ways to keep your body feeling alive and fully expressive. If you wish to be a triple threat, study song and dance extensively because musical theatre is where the work often is. Basic ballet not only offers a classical personal presentation but will make it easier working with choreographers, who tend to employ ballet terminology no matter what the style of dance they are staging. Jazz and other popular forms such as hip hop keep you connected with the rhythms of contemporary culture. Dance improvisation allows great risk taking without the pressure of dialogue. Contact improvisation increases your understanding of kinesthetic relationships. Historic dance classes provide you with the basics for the pavane, galliard, brawle, minuet, gavotte, hornpipe, quadrille, polonaise and other forms revealing great insight into various classical periods.

Mime—While mime is not at present a popular form of training or performance, it is well worth your time should an opportunity to study it present itself because of the intense concentration, precision, selectivity and detail that go into the art. You have neither the burden nor crutch of words or any sounds. Without set pieces and usually without props, you get to, in fact must, create the universe around you, so a wind does not exist until you are blown away by it, a wall does not exist until you create it by bumping against it and a table does not exist until you lean into air to define it. You need to make others see what is totally invisible. The result is unparalleled sharpness and stunning specificity.

Combat—Any actor interested in physical theatre must study stage combat. All drama is conflict, which frequently escalates into violence, but must be done without endangering participants. Training includes unarmed combat skills such as illusory slaps, shoves, punches, kicks, taking a fall, throwing and holding methods, armed adaptations of fencing, rapier and dagger, short sword, broadsword, quarterstaff, mace, battle axe, spear, club, shields and knives, plus sports like wrestling and martial arts. Training at all levels is available all the way up to certification from the Society of Fight Masters.

Mask—Unlike dance and mime which eliminate talk, mask work removes human facial expression. Training in this area began with Jacques Copeau at the Théâtre du Vieux-Colombier in 1913, though mask performance has always permeated history and cultures. Actors may first study the notion of "neutral" and what that might mean for movement and characterization, then work through a range of increasingly defined masks to a complete "complex character" mask. Some productions, for example of ancient Greek tragedies, employ masks even today. If you are an actor who relies heavily on your facial expressions but are not as fully inventive and fluid in the use of the rest of your body, this is a crucial area of study for you.

A Reading Menu

A great deal of further independent study is available to you through the following texts. It does not matter where you decide to begin as long as you make a commitment that you will always be reading something from this bountiful list of sources:

GENERAL ACTING TEXTS WITH APPROACHES TO MOVEMENT:

Annie Loui, *The Physical Actor: Exercises for Action and Awareness* (Routledge, 2009)

A comprehensive set of exercises, designed for the development of a strong and flexible physical body able to move with ease through space and interact instinctively onstage. The reader is guided through a full course of movement skills, from daily warm-up to effective partnering, spatial awareness and fine motor control through mime, heightened co-ordination and sustained motion.

Michael Lugering, *The Expressive Actor: Integrated Voice, Movement and Acting Training* (Routledge, 2012)

A foundational, preparatory training method, using movement to unlock the entire acting process. Its action-based perspective integrates voice, movement and basic acting training into a unified approach. A wealth of exercises and diagrams guide the reader through a step-by-step course for both solo and classroom use, in which voice and body training become the central prerequisite to actor training.

Nicole Potter, *Movement for Actors* (Allworth Press, 2002)

Experts in a wide array of disciplines provide insights into the Alexander technique, the use of psychological gesture, period movement, Laban work, postmodern choreography and Suzuki training, among others. This collection is valuable to all readers looking for stimulation and new approaches, offering a practical master class on movement from the Head of Movement at the Royal Academy of Dramatic Art.

Jackie Snow, *Movement Training for Actors* (Bloomsbury Methuen Drama, 2013)

A complete curriculum on movement training: from pure movement to games, Grotowski, Alexander, ballet, yoga and Feldenkreis. Snow guides readers through practical steps, enabling the actor to master each technique and apply it to performance and character. The DVD contains examples performed by acting students and a series of three mini master classes.

Melissa Hurt, *Arthur Lessac's Embodied Actor Training* (Routledge, 2014)

The work of renowned voice and movement trainer Arthur Lessac is placed in the context of contemporary actor training. Lessac's practice of embodied acting, a key subject in contemporary performance, is explored, with guides for the actor to experience both skill and expression as a subjective whole through active meditation and spatial attunement. The book feeds a wider discussion of embodiment, as well as providing concrete examples of how the practice can be put into effect, enhanced by interviews conducted with Lessac and his master teachers.

Moni Yakim, *Creating a Character: A Physical Approach to Acting* (Applause, 2000)

For several decades Moni Yakim has taught his unique blend of physical training and emotional exploration to a generation of American actors that include Meryl Streep, Sigourney Weaver and Kevin Kline. Herein, his acting process is available to all actors and theater professionals. The book defines different characters as basic archetypes, or "selves": The Vulnerable Self, The Trusting Self, The Instinctive Self. It then goes on to list ways of developing these Selves from a purely physical standpoint.

Theresa Mitchell, *Movement: From Person to Actor to Character* (Scarecrow Press, 1998)

A concise collection of common movement principles, such as use of breath, alignment, relaxation, imagery and surroundings. Illustrations provide knowledge of the human body and function, serving as a foundation for advanced movement techniques. Case studies outline a variety of characterization projects from well-known plays, to further illustrate exercises within the text.

Fay Thompson and Michael Howard, *The Lucid Body: A Guide for the Physical Actor* (Allworth, 2008)

Rooted in explorations of the seven chakra energy centers, this text reveals how each body holds the possibility of every human condition. Through energy analysis, this program shows how to use physical training to create characters from all walks of life—however cruel, desolate or neurotic—expanding an actor's emotional and physical range.

Vanessa Ewan and Debbie Green, *Actor Movement: Expression of a Physical Being* (Bloomsbury Methuen Drama, 2015)

Great actors are not simply skilled interpreters of text, but also of movement, able to embody all aspects of a character's life. A textbook and DVD resource for actors and their guides, helping performers to become many bodies, all behaving differently from their own, aiding them to construct, inhabit and offer each character, with its multiplicity of known and unknown physical expression.

PHYSICAL THEATRE METHODS:

Edited by Simon Murray and John Keefe, *Physical Theatres: A Critical Introduction* (Routledge, 2007)

The first comprehensive overview of non-text-based theatre, from experimental dance to traditional mime, this book synthesizes the history, theory and practice of physical theatre for students and performers. Insisting that there are many physical theatres and arguing for the essential physicality of all theatrical forms, the book not only examines the acknowledged luminaries of physical theatre, but also forges a new lens through which the practices of recent exciting dramatists and theatre makers can be viewed.

Andrei Droznin (author), Paul Allon (editor), *Andrei Droznin's Physical Training: A Russian Master Class* (Routledge, 2012)

A unique introduction to the master teacher behind a program of stage movement training taught all over the world. Droznin's extensive influence on the way biomechanical principles and the relationship between mind and body are approached in modern drama schools is herein finally documented, with both his methods and the motivation behind them.

Giuliano Campo and Zygmunt Molik, *Voice and Body Work: The Legacy of Jerzey Grotowski* (Routledge, 2010)

One of the original members of Grotowski's acting company, Molik explores the unique development of voice and body exercises throughout his career in actor training. Constructed from conversations between Molik and the author, it provides insight into his methodology and focuses on his 'Body Alphabet' system for actors, allowing them to combine both voice and body in their preparatory process.

Jade Rosina McCutcheon, *Awakening the Performing Body* (Rodopi, 2008)

Practice-based research presented in a pedagogical format, this text is a guide for acting teachers who wish to pursue a more spiritual approach to acting and participate in the goal of reclaiming the sacred in theatre, as well as those who seek a more body centered and imaginative approach to character and actor–audience connections.

MASK AND MIME:

Dymphna Callery, *Through the Body: A Practical Guide to Physical Theatre* (Nick Hern Press, 2014)

Callery introduces the principles behind the work of key twentieth-century theatre practitioners (Artaud, Grotowski, Meyerhold, Brook and Lecoq, among others) and offers exercises by which their theories can be turned into practice and their principles explored in action. A series of workshops include preparing the body through Awareness, Articulation, Energy and Neutrality, Mask-work and an investigation of Presence, Complicité, Play, Audience, Rhythm, Sound and Emotion.

Alexander Iliev, *Towards a Theory of Mime* (Routledge, 2014)

A unique book about non-verbal communication and performance, combining a broad global history of the evolution of human communication with an introduction to the general practice of mime. Iliev traces a lineage from Marceau and Barrault to his own distinguished practice as performer and teacher.

Claude Kipnis, *The Mime Book* (Meriwether, 1988)

The great French mime performer Kipnis reveals the mechanisms and techniques of mime in an easy-to-understand translation, which is not a theoretical "art of" book, but a functional "how to" and "why to" instructional guide. Individual exercises include detailed coverage of body movements, the illusion and how to create a world. A comprehensive explanation of how the functions of mime are achieved.

Libby Appel, *Mask Characterization: An Acting Process* (Southern Illinois Press, 1982)

Behind the mask, Appel notes, students are free to create a personality; paradoxically, because the mask hides the self, it enables students to probe more deeply into themselves. The book provides the theory behind exercises and the step-by-step procedure to develop character from masks. Divided into two parts, The Instructor's Guide and The Actor's Guide, it also includes an introductory chapter explaining mask characterization in the classroom, and a sample class schedule.

Sears Eldredge, *Mask Improvisation for Actor Training and Performance* (Northwestern University Press, 1996)

Because mask improvisation is relatively new in American theatre training, this work is designed to acquaint readers with the theories and techniques of the method. It gives a historical survey of the role of masks in various cultures. The book examines the beliefs surrounding the "transformative" qualities attributed to masks and traces their theatrical uses through significant eras. A wide range of activities and exercises are provided.

Eli Simon, *Masking Unmasked: Four Approaches to Basic Acting* (Palgrave Macmillan, 2003)

A basic guide to using mask to develop character and movement. Four sections correspond to mask size: Full-Face, Clowning, Bag and Half-Face masks. Each addresses basic acting principles and shows how ancient technique can be applied to contemporary performance. Actors in masks are required to tap into profound physical, vocal, emotional and psychological transformations in creating a character, promoting honest, believable and detailed work. Illustrated profusely, hands-on exercises demonstrate how to shift cleanly between beats, execute specificity, unleash creative impulses, take risks and expand character range, power and vulnerability.

STAGE COMBAT:

Dale Anthony Girard, *Actors on Guard: A Practical Guide for the Use of the Rapier and Dagger for Stage and Screen* (Routledge, 2014)

The most comprehensive guide to the art of theatrical swordplay available provides the reader with historical, theoretical and practical bases for learning, practicing and presenting theatrical sword fights. Focusing specifically on the Elizabethan rapier and dagger (the most popular weapons used in stage fights), it provides the skills and knowledge essential to presenting safe and effective fights, for both stage and screen.

J.D. Martinez and Caren Caraway, *Combat Mime: A Non-violent Approach to Stage Combat* (Rowan and Littlefield, 1982)

This book outlines in simple terms and with illustrations how to safely create illusions of unarmed stage violence. Aiming to help prevent injuries related to stage fights, it is intended for actors, directors or stage managers who are new to stage violence; however, experienced fight choreographers may find new techniques as well.

Jenn Boughn, *Fisticuffs, Stunts and Swordplay for Theatre and Film* (Allworth Press, 2006)

This comprehensive guide covers everything needed to stage believable, safe action for theatre and other performing arts. From basic falls, rolls and tumbling to punches, kicks, hair pulls and head slams to advanced handling of weapons, in-depth instruction is provided for realistic-looking fights and physical comedy, including grappling, slapping, pushing and choking.

Also included are basic drills for the quarterstaff, European rapier and Japanese katana-style swordplay. Complete with illustrations and step-by-step directions.

Jonathan Howell, *Stage Fighting: A Practical Guide* (Crowood Press, 2009)

The practicalities of choreographing realistic fight scenes on stage are revealed in a way that is both convincing for the audience and safe for the actors. A wide range of combat is explored, from ritualized swordplay to the slaps and punches of a bar-room brawl.

Braun McAsh, *Fight Choreography: A Practical Guide to Stage, Film, and Television* (Crowood Press, 2011)

Fight scenes must tell the story of the fight in a way that is safe for the performer—to do this, the choreographer has to consider everything that directly impinges on physical movement. This manual looks at sets, costumes, lighting, special effects, the variety of armor and weapons and how to choreograph fights with phrases, logic and rhythm. It gives specific advice on subjects from symbolism to blood effects and from battle scenes to motion capture, explaining the artistic process of creating a fight scene from scripted page to finished performance.

EMBODIED COGNITION BASED ON NEUROSCIENCE RESEARCH:

Rich Kemp, *Embodied Acting: What Neuroscience Tells Us about Performance* (Routledge, 2012)

A pragmatic examination of how recent discoveries within cognitive science can—and should—be applied to performance. For too long, a conceptual separation of mind and body has dominated actor training in the West. Cognitive science has shown this binary to be illusory, shattering the traditional boundaries between mind and body, reason and emotion, knowledge and imagination. This volume explores the impact that a more holistic approach to the "bodymind" can have on the acting process.

Rhonda Blair, *The Actor, Image, and Action: Acting and Cognitive Neuroscience* (Routledge, 2007)

The first full-length study of actor training using the insights of cognitive neuroscience. In an innovative reassessment of both the practice and theory of acting, Blair examines the physiological relationship between bodily action and emotional experience. In doing so, she provides a further step in Stanislavski's attempts to help the actor "reach the unconscious by conscious means."

Robert Barton, *Acting Reframes* (Routledge, 2011)

The use of NLP (Neuro Linguistic Programming) is presented to the reader in a playful, creative and accessible style, structured to enable solo study as well as group work. The text offers a range of engaging exercises and extensive analysis of language patterns used in performance. It is a source for enhancing communication between all theatre practitioners in training, productions and daily life outside the theatre.

PERIOD STYLE ACTING TEXTS WITH SIGNIFICANT MOVEMENT FOCUS:

Maria Aitken, *Style: Acting in High Comedy* (Applause Books, 1996)

Rather than a critical examination of high comedy, this is a collection of suggestions for the middlemen: the actors who have to catch the comic spark from the playwright and pass it on to the audience. The effort involved must be imperceptible: one has to acquire the cleverness, the articulacy, the "febrility" of the characters and then make the whole laborious exercise seem like swimming through silk. Aitken stresses that characters in high comedies don't find verbal sophistication difficult or unfamiliar; they enjoy it as you might enjoy slang.

Robert Barton, *Style for Actors* (Routledge, 2011)

The past is a foreign country, and this book (winner of the American Theatre in Higher Education's Best Book Award) explores it from the actor's point of view. Specific guides range from Greek, Elizabethan, Restoration and Georgian theatre to more contemporary stylings, including Futurism, Surrealism and Postmodernism. The text presents the actor with roles and genres that will most commonly confront them and with analysis moving from entire genres to specific scenes and characters. Nearly 150 practical exercises offer a newfound understanding of style to make the leap from page to performance.

Simon Callow, *Acting in Restoration Comedy* (Applause Books, 1991)

The art of acting in restoration comedy, the buoyant, often bawdy romps which celebrated the reopening of the English theatres after Cromwell's dour reign, is the subject of Simon Callow's lively investigation. Callow, one of Britain's foremost actors, aims to restore the form to all its original voluptuous vigor, showing the way to attain clarity and hilarity in some of the most delightful roles ever conceived for the theatre.

Jerry L. Crawford, Catherine Hurst and Michael Lugering, *Acting in Person and in Style* (Brown & Benchmark Publishers, 1995)

The authors define the personalization process as one in which the actor discovers and explores, in the self, characteristics, qualities, attitudes and experiences that are legitimate dimensions of the role being created. The book then makes suggestions for moving into less immediately familiar periods and styles.

John Harrop and Sabin R. Epstein, *Acting with Style* (Prentice Hall, 1990)

A guide to the process of approaching style plays with useful facts, data, information and exercises, and offers an accessible writing style that expresses a sensitivity to the needs of actors. In addition to presenting the physical approach to actor training, the authors encourage readers to use text and concepts with creativity and imagination, asserting that the process of discovering language is not limited to one specific time, place or culture.

Lyn Oxenford, *Playing Period Plays* (Coach House Press, 1966)

Deals with the simple stage aspects of producing and acting period plays. The spirit of the age, the style of acting, costume, manners and dance, and music are some of the subjects covered. Suggestions are also made for adaptation of the material for pageant and arena work.

Suzanne Ramczyk, *Delicious Dissembling: A Compleat Guide to Performing Restoration Comedy* (Heinemann, 2003)

Restoration comedies of manners are at once bitingly true-to-life and deceptively artificial. Their style, elegance, grace and wit provide the kind of challenge actors continue to love. Ramczyk offers both directors and actors the tools they need to perform these popular plays.

Bari Rolfe, *Movement for Period Plays* (Personabooks, 1985)

Suggestions are offered for creating movement suitable to the era of period plays set in the Greek/Roman, Medieval/Early Tudor, Elizabethan/Jacobean, Restoration, Eighteenth Century, Romantic and Victorian/Edwardian eras. Includes discussions of clothing and how it affected movement, customs and manners, salutations and dances.

Janet Suzman, *Acting in Shakespearean Comedy* (Applause Books, 1990)

Suzman presents some well-crafted lessons on how actors should approach performing Shakespeare in this book, which has a related DVD. Includes a masterful examination of the differences between tragedy and comedy. Meaty advice and anecdotal wisdom about acting comedy from a veteran Shakespearean performer.

BODY LANGUAGE/KINESICS BOOKS:

Barbara Pease and Allen Pease, *The Definitive Book of Body Language* (Random House, 2008)

While it is a scientific fact that people's gestures give away their true intentions, most of us do not know how to read body language—and do not realize how our own physical movements speak to others. These kinesics experts share techniques for reading body signals. Drawing on recent research from evolutionary biology, psychology and medical technologies, the authors examine each component of body language and provide basic vocabulary to recognize attitudes and emotions through behavior.

Merlyn Cundiff, *Kinesics: The Power of Silent Command* (Simon & Shuster, 2002)

Provides a detailed discussion of kinesics or physical relationships between people as well as how to incorporate this knowledge into your daily life. A treatment of different ways people communicate, including body language, gestures, expressions, reactions and other non-verbal means, drawing heavily on descriptive communications.

Janine Driver and Mariska van Aalst, *You Say More Than You Think* (Harmony, 2011)

With a keen eye, Driver reveals methods that other experts refuse to share with the public, and debunks major myths other experts swear are fact, offering a seven day plan and seven second solutions to turn any interpersonal situation to your advantage.

Tonya Reiman, *The Power of Body Language* (Gallery Books, 2008)

A practical, personal playbook for zoning in on what others are saying to you without words, revealing the hidden meaning behind specific gestures, facial cues, stances and body movements, offering potential life-changing, career-saving, trouble-shooting skills.

David Lambert, *Body Language 101* (Skyhorse Publishing, 2008)

Aiming to help you become a veritable human lie detector, spotting exactly when people are telling the truth, when they are lying and how they are feeling. Analyzing clues from folded arms, the distance away someone stands when talking to you, facial expressions and blinking eyes, Lambert provides insights into comprehending any culture and knowing more about friends, spouse, colleagues, lovers, competitors and enemies.

Marvin Karlins, *What Every Body Is Saying* (William Morrow, 2008)

Navarro, a former FBI counterintelligence officer in nonverbal behavior, explains how to "speed-read" people: decode sentiments and behaviors, avoid hidden pitfalls and look for deceptive behaviors. He also analyzes how your body language can influence what your boss, family, friends and strangers think of you.

Ray R. Birdwhistell, *Kinesics and Context* (University of Pennsylvania Press, 2007)

In this study of human body motion or kinesics, the author advances the theory that human communication needs and uses all the senses, that the information conveyed by human gestures and movements is coded and patterned differently in various cultures, and that these codes can be discovered by skilled scrutiny of particular movements within a social context.

Preparing for Media Work

If you want to work professionally, you should be as prepared to face a camera as a live audience. More and more frequently, actors are onscreen before they are onstage. The professional union for screen actors (Screen Actors Guild, SAG) has three times as many members as that for stage actors (Actors Equity Association, AEA). A host of books and instructional videos on acting for the camera are available. Start with the following four, which offer sound advice on making peace with the lens, studio processes and simply being a good actor:

Robert Benedetti, *Action! Acting for Film and Television.* Needham Heights, MA: Allyn & Bacon, 2001. A short handbook, clear, concise and easy to follow. Divided into two parts: (1) Working with the Camera and (2) Preparing Yourself and Your Role. Offers exercises for you and a friend working with a home camera.

Michael Caine, *Acting in Film.* New York: Applause, 1990. Though the oldest source listed here, it is also still the best. Caine is the consummate production-proof actor, always good even when he is acting opposite muppets or sharks. His careful, personal instruction is clear, humble and empathetic. (Both book and DVD are available.)

Mel Churcher, *Acting for Film.* London: Virgin Books, 2003. A longer, more in-depth examination by a former British actor, who has served as an acting coach on films around the world, this book offers an international and a woman's perspective on the process. Full of entertaining anecdotes.

Mel Churcher, *A Screen Acting Workshop.* London: Nick Hern Books Limited, 2011. A series of five workshops taking actors through the process of "creating, developing and delivering assured performances onscreen." The text is accompanied by a 90 minute DVD demonstrating the techniques put forth by the author.

More and more student films are made each year. Watch for notices of chances to get involved in these bare-bones projects that help you adjust to the camera without adding in the entire studio and massive production team distractions.

Camera comfort is a worthwhile endeavor, especially if you are not a "video baby" whose every major transition has been recorded by your family. And even if you are, it is quite different to adjust to seeing yourself perform a character other than the one you evolved in your household over the years. If you have regular access to a camera, use it as a rehearsal tool for acting class projects.

With the increased sophistication of the technology of video games and the technique of motion capture, actors are involved as both the voice and movement template for characters in video games. The motion capture labs are similar to green screen environments that require actors to imagine the location of the story. As the computer is capturing your physical actions for manipulation into a game character, you will need to be prepared to repeat gestures more than once. This requires a kinesthetic memory and patience.

Games rely on actors who have well developed physical imaginations and can evolve with their character as the game evolves. The change in technology has also caused acting within video games to become a serious business, with agents advertising online for actors to interview for roles in games. Some actors such as Mark Hamill have made a career in the game world and become noted for the roles they have created.

Advanced Training Inquiries

If you decide you want to focus more on movement after you graduate from your present program or your independent review of material in this book and may want to seek advanced training, how can you evaluate the strength of various movement programs? Here are some signposts you can look for. Use them as you read the material you receive and are encouraged to watch. Check for answers. If you do not find them there, be sure to ask during your interview. Try to meet not just those in official positions, but with students now in the program. You do not wish to commit two or three years of your life without a sense of what you are getting into.

- What is the breadth of the program? Does it favor one distinct movement system to the exclusion of others?
- How many full-time instructors do they have? What are their backgrounds, degrees, certifications?
- Whom do the teachers credit as their major influences?
- Do the faculty work as movement coaches on productions? What is the degree to which the movement and acting programs are integrated?
- What physical relaxation/alignment/focus approaches are taught, and how do they integrate them with the rest of movement instruction?

- What is the percentage of text related activity to organic exploration in the training? How often are you likely to be working with a scripted character vs. general work not focused on specific characterization?
- How much, if any, time is devoted to the tangential disciplines, such as combat, dance, mime and mask?
- How much of the training appears to be external in approach and how much is actually fully somatic?
- How much time will you have in any one class? How often do movement classes meet and for what duration?
- What is the progression of classes over the course of the degree or program?
- How large are the classes? Do they include private tutorials?
- How is student movement competence tested and evaluated?

Review and Renew

You might launch your movement future by going back through the chapters of this book to check in with yourself about where you are regarding awareness offered and journeys suggested. How have your self-analyses from Chapter 1 changed over the recent months? What answers would be different with the passage of time? In what ways does the body anatomy knowledge from Chapter 2 influence your choices in daily life in your carriage and extensions, and how has it changed the way you approach a character, adjusting your body to the demands of the role? Have you investigated any of the paths offered in Chapter 3? If not, where do you think you might start if time allows? How are you integrating the psychophysical methods offered in Chapter 4 and the character analysis approaches from Chapter 5 into your performance preparation? How has your knowledge and intuitive sense of the acting space delineated in Chapter 6 and that of the audience beyond expanded from this discussion? How are you more of a master of these spaces? What is the most stylized theatre experience you have had of late? What did you recognize and appreciate for your new found style knowledge from Chapter 7? In what ways do you feel more ready for the challenge? In each of the above areas, not only identify where you have made progress but consider setting some further development goals.

EXERCISE 8.1 **SECOND CHECK**

1. Self-Check—Write down the number of each chapter and then a short sentence about how you are perceiving and performing differently as a result of that information. Add a second sentence about how you intend to move forward to even greater knowledge.
2. Imitation Check—If you are in a class where an imitation was assigned for Chapter 1, return to that project with the same partners. Ask the same questions for the persons you are imitating, first from your own observation and then by interviewing them to compare their perceptions with yours. Prepare a brief theatrical presentation in which you demonstrate a before and after, showing your partner at the beginning of the term and then now.

The ability to manipulate your body to make your desired impression is a powerful tool, both onstage and off. In your theatre work, such capacity gives you genuine control and poise counterbalanced with imaginative and surprising choices. And with that skill and risk blend comes freedom. It leads you to genuine versatility and the power to delineate each character with exacting detail. In daily life, it offers you the capacity to interact more successfully in encounters with friends and strangers. It protects you from leaving a false impression due to misinterpreted body language. It simply allows you to feel more in control. We hope *Movement: Onstage and Off* has provided you with insights and tools and wish you a hugely successful journey.

Summary

If you wish to become a real actor, meticulous research and experimentation into every dimension of the physical lives of your characters is essential. Regular practice in the areas of aerobics, strength, flexibility, focus, coordination, composure and imagination will keep your instrument primed and ready and it is helpful to supplement traditional actor training with specialized, tangential movement disciplines. A considerable bibliography offers you the opportunity to study all areas of movement independently. Awareness of specific preparation for media performance is crucial because that is often where the work is. It is never too early to begin to consider the kind of advanced training you may wish to pursue. In your continuing journey toward movement mastery, it matters less what you are doing than that you are always doing something.

Finding Fitness

Fitness amounts to a state of health and well-being, the ability to function efficiently and effectively, adjusting to various physical challenges. A fit actor has a strengthened immune system preventing chronic conditions, a reduced risk of injury, better sleep, more elevated moods, blood pressure control, weight control, better posture and improved neuropsychological function. Physical fitness often leads to mental, social and emotional fitness as well, plus greater strength, agility, balance, coordination, power and a faster reaction time. It allows you to perform everyday tasks without undue fatigue and increases your quality of life. Who wouldn't want all that? Oh, and did we mention it can help you become a better actor?

The Fitness Five

There are five basic elements that lead to overall fitness. They are tested separately, though often overlap in practical application, and progress in one can strongly influence growth in another.

1. CARDIOVASCULAR

This is how efficiently your heart and lungs provide fuel, in the form of blood and oxygen, to your tissues and cells to sustain continuous movement. You can track your heart rate while performing continuous movement using large muscle groups, such as running on a treadmill, jogging, elliptical training, walking, swimming, rowing, dancing, biking, endurance sports like soccer or basketball, or interval training. Aerobic assessments measure distances traveled or the time taken to complete a specified distance, while aiming for the fullest possible range of motion. Cardio is often identified as the single most important fitness component, because exercise that raises your heart rate helps strengthen its ability to pump blood efficiently, and when the vascular and respiratory systems work smoothly together, your muscles are able to best utilize all the energy available to them.

2. STRENGTH

Muscular fitness is based on the ability of your muscles to exert force to overcome resistance. Muscle strength can be measured by the amount of force needed to overcome maximal resistance in an exercise in one effort. An example is the amount of weight that can be lifted in a one-repetition bench press. Keeping muscle fitness and tone helps you to avoid injuries to your body's joints, because your muscles become more flexible and have the ability to deal with the stress you place upon and around your joints.

3. ENDURANCE

This category moves beyond the amount of weight that can be lifted or moved, to how long you can repetitively contract a group of muscles. Build muscle endurance by performing many repetitions of a lower resistance exercise with a less than maximal amount of force. An example is the number of pushups that can be performed using your body weight as resistance. Optimal strength and endurance help to increase muscle mass, improve posture and alignment, and reduce the risk of back problems and joint injuries.

4. FLEXIBILITY

Joint mobility involves the range of motion of your joints, surrounding muscles and connective tissue. Evaluations, such as the sit and reach, are based on the distance that your body covers while performing stretches. If sitting with your legs extended in front, extending your upper body towards your feet, you can touch your toes, your hamstrings, the large muscles along the back of your thighs, are flexible. A lack of flexibility can stop you from doing things in your daily life and inhibit your other fitness goals; many athletes work on flexibility despite the fact that their sport may focus on strength or endurance. A full range of motion makes cardiovascular activities feel easier. Body awareness is also a strong influencer of how you move, your confidence in your physical abilities and your appreciation for your unique strengths and challenges.

5. BODY COMPOSITION

Compare lean body mass to body fat to determine body composition. This element of fitness is often misinterpreted as simply weight or physical size. A more accurate assessment is leanness, the ratio of muscle to fat. Assessments are based on the percentage of body fat to total body weight. Recommended body fat percentages range from 14 to 25 percent for women and 9 to 19 percent for men. Muscle-to-fat ratio (leanness) can be measured by underwater weighing and dual energy x-ray absorptiometry. Sufficient muscle mass is vital for the well-being of your bones and to keep your heart healthy. So rather than focusing solely on the weight you see when you step on a scale, consider your muscle-to-fat ratio.

> *I encourage you to "date" every kind of exercise. There is something active out there that you would love to do.*
>
> **Chris Powell, trainer and author**

Ten Training Tips

These are the fitness suggestions, garnered from a range of publications, that have given the greatest number of people the greatest success.

1. Search until you find exercises that you enjoy physically and mentally, something from each category that is actually satisfying to do.
2. Figure out whether you work best in team activity, alone or with an exercise buddy who will keep you motivated. Figure out the time of day and circumstances under which you are likely to keep at it—all of your optimal conditions.
3. Branch out beyond one specific form of exercise to enhance your overall fitness and athletic performance. Shake it up through the concept of FITT (frequency, intensity, time and type), varying type and increasing frequency, intensity or time every couple of weeks.
4. Start with simple goals and then progress to longer range ones. Make them realistic and achievable. A short-term goal might be to walk 10 minutes a day three days a week, intermediate to walk 30 minutes five days a week, long-term to complete a 5K walk.
5. Keep it fun. If you're not enjoying your workouts, try something different. Join a volleyball or softball league. Take a ballroom dancing class. Check out a health club or martial arts center. You're more likely to stick with a program if you're enjoying yourself.
6. Make it part of your daily routine. Schedule workouts as you would any other important activity. You can also slip in physical activity throughout the day. Take the stairs instead of the elevator. Pedal a stationary bike or do strength training exercises while you watch TV at night.
7. Put it on paper. Are you hoping to lose weight? Boost your energy? Sleep better? Manage a chronic condition? Write it down. Seeing the benefits on paper may help you stay motivated. You may find it helps to keep an exercise diary, recording what you did during each session, how long you exercised and how you felt afterward. Recording your efforts can remind you when you need it that you're making progress.
8. Reward yourself. After each exercise session, take a few minutes to savor the good feelings that exercise gives you. When you reach a longer range goal, treat yourself to a new pair of walking shoes or new tunes to enjoy while you exercise.
9. Be flexible. If you're too busy to work out or simply don't feel up to it, take a day or two off. Be gentle with yourself if you need a break. The important thing is to get back on track as soon as you can.
10. Leave your procrastinating, unmotivated self behind. Let your fearless, confident, positive, motivated and dedicated self step up.

Heart Rates

Determine your level of aerobic endurance by the three following heart rates. Take your pulse rate by locating the pulse on your wrist or neck artery. Count the pulse for six seconds and add a zero to get your pulse rate.

Resting Heart Rate

Many factors can influence resting heart rate, including temperature, humidity, previous activity, emotions, time since eating, fatigue and illness. People who have high levels of aerobic fitness have a lower resting heart rate and a quicker recovery time than people with less aerobic fitness. The best time to determine your resting heart rate is to take your pulse before you get out of bed in the morning.

Working Heart Rate

There are various rates: 60 to 90 beats per minute is an extremely light to a very light level of exertion that is associated with the warm-up or cool-down phase of aerobic activity. 100–150 beats per minute is the training zone for your heart. Between 100 and 130 beats per minute, you still burn fat, and yet you can breathe and speak easily. As your heart rate moves into the 140–150 zone, you are moving beyond the training zone and as a consequence you are sweating more and starting to have trouble carrying on a conversation. At over 160 beats per minute your body reverses the aerobic process to protect itself from stress. This approximates the endurance of a competitive athlete. Your breathing is labored (you can't talk) and the muscles are burning. It is similar to if you had just done the 100 yard dash.

Recovery Heart Rate

This measurement is taken five minutes after you have slowed the activity. After five minutes, your pulse should not exceed 120. If it does, you know you are overextending yourself, so simply continue to walk slowly and stretch until the rate is 120 or less. Ten minutes after exercising it should be below 100. If not, you should cut back on the intensity with which you exercise. At your next workout, move less vigorously by walking more, running less and using your arms less energetically.

Rate of Perceived Exertion

This is a way of becoming involved in the experience of your heart rate to determine your aerobic level. Instead of focusing on your pulse rate, you concentrate on the experience of your activity. You will want to note your reaction to different types of activity and to different amounts of exertion.

Know Your Capacity

The first rule of aerobics is: Never get ahead of yourself. Rushing just doesn't work and only invites trouble. Work up to your goals gradually, not only to accustom the heart to new demands but also to let tendons and muscles adjust themselves to the new activity. Indications that you are overdoing your exercise are: a feeling of tightness or pain in your chest, severe breathlessness, dizziness, losing control of your muscles and nausea. Any one of these symptoms is a clear signal to stop exercising immediately. Shortness of breath an hour and a half later is another indication of overexertion. By comparison, the normal breath rate at rest ranges from 12 to 16 breaths per minute.

EXERCISE B.1 **HEART RATE, ENDURANCE, SELF-KNOWLEDGE**

1. Whenever pursuing aerobic activity, take time to check in with each of the categories above.
2. Prior to the activity or earlier in the day, take your resting heart rate.
3. Stop at various points during activity to check your working heart rate.
4. Wait five minutes after finishing and gauge your recovery heart rate.
5. Analyze your perceived level of exertion.
6. Periodically check in with yourself regarding any changes or developments in your overall capacity.

Index